51
DEREK JARMAN
FERGUSON & Co Ltd

← Derek Jarman wearing his *Money Cape* in front of his Bankside studio, London, 1970
Derek Jarman with his *Sky Capes* on the wall, Bankside studio, London, 1971

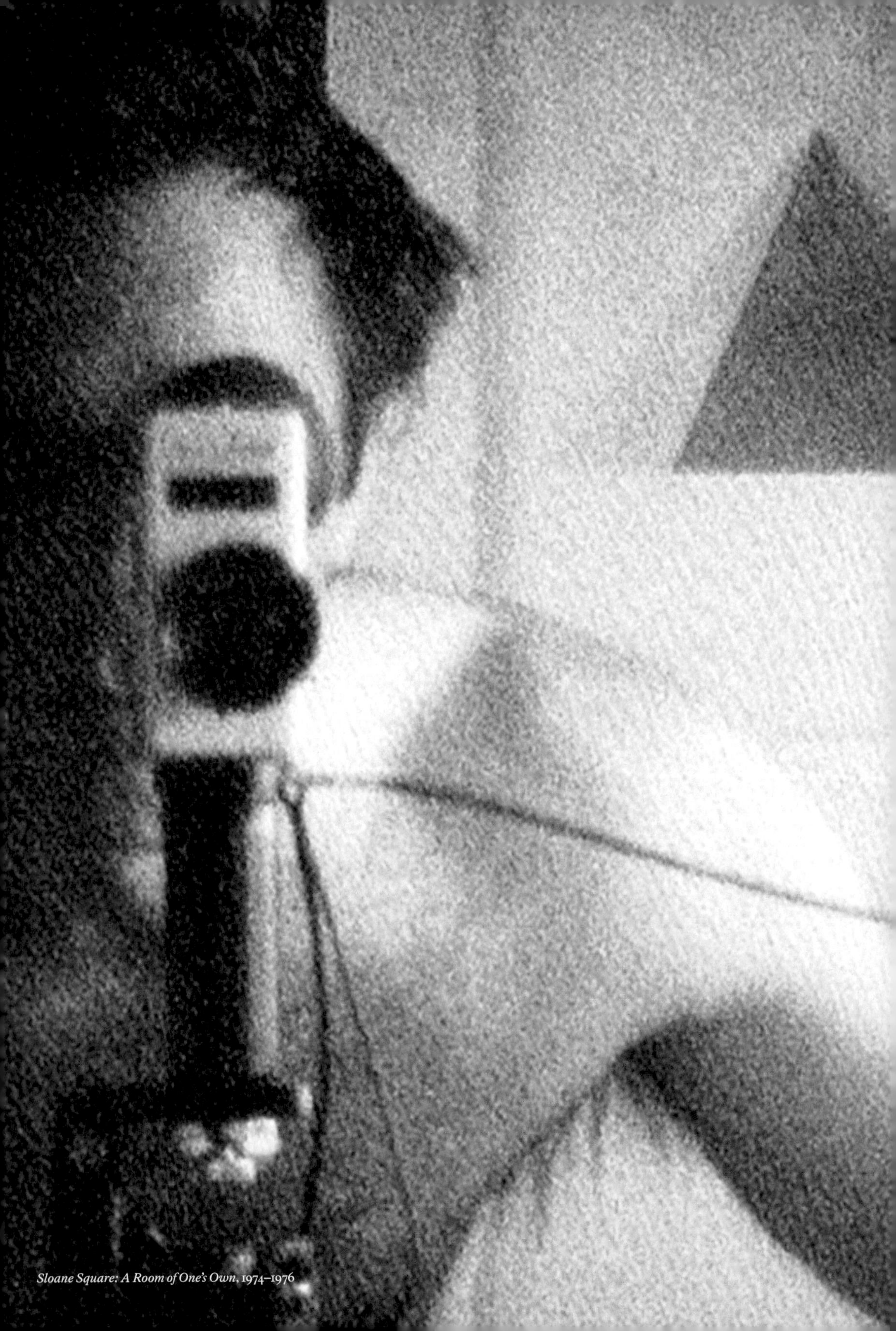

Sloane Square: A Room of One's Own, 1974–1976

Derek Jarman, Third Eye Centre, Glasgow, 1989

Derek Jarman, Richard Salmon studio, London, 1992

DEREK JARMAN

jrp|editions

PARADISES OF DUNGENESS

CLAIRE LE RESTIF

PAGES 12–14: Derek Jarman in *Blue*, 1993

If you have a garden and a library,
you have everything you need.[1]
—Cicero

1 'Si hortum in bibliotheca habes, deerit nihil', Cicero, 'To Varro', *Ad familiares*, IX, 4.

2 Vinciane Despret, *Au bonheur des morts. Récits de ceux qui restent*, La Découverte, Paris 2015, p. 14.

3 Derek Jarman, *Modern Nature: The Journals of Derek Jarman* [1991], Vintage Classics, London 2018.

Derek Jarman (1942–1994) is regarded in the United Kingdom as the figurehead of the British underground scene of the 1980s and 1990s, and this recognition is now gradually spreading from continental Europe to North America. Artist, film director, screenwriter, writer, gardener, drag performer with a love of the music hall, gay rights activist, he left his mark on a defining moment in European culture. It is to his artistic and political position that the Centre d'Art Contemporain d'Ivry–Le Crédac wanted to pay tribute with the exhibition dedicated to him in the autumn of 2021.

We felt it was essential to highlight the living work of a deceased artist, which bears messages that are as intimate as they are collective. As Vinciane Despret reminds us, 'if we don't take care of them, the dead die completely [...] It falls upon us to offer them more life.'[2] Jarman was part of a queer community, and the exhibition was a reminder that if society is making progress, it is often thanks to minorities, and that the fight against homophobia continues to this day. When he found out he was HIV-positive in 1986, Jarman put all his energy into denouncing the impact of AIDS on his community and on his own life, through the content of his oeuvre, the affirmation of a singular aesthetic and the absolute need to make the autobiographical universal simultaneously.

Entitled *Dead Souls Whisper (1986–1993)*, the exhibition brought together some 50 works produced between the time Jarman was diagnosed as HIV-positive and his death. Some of his Super-8 films from the mid-1970s were shown alongside paintings and assemblages created during the latter part of his life. This period coincided with the time when he brought to life his legendary garden around Prospect Cottage in Dungeness in Kent, the creation of which proved to be a therapy, a metaphor for his relentless battle for life, and a garden of 'modern nature' – to use the title of a book by the artist[3] – able to combat crises. The garden was not a melancholy refuge, but a genuine place of creation. While it may not have been materially represented in the Crédac exhibition, it was indeed omnipresent.

When I visited Prospect Cottage for the first time in June 2019, in the company of Amanda Wilkinson,[4] it was undoubtedly the garden, which had piqued my curiosity ever since I first read a text by Jarman a few years earlier, I had come to see.[5] I looked up at the little painted cottage, with its yellow door and window frames, kept just as Jarman had found it one spring afternoon in 1986. To protect it from the sun and the violent, moisture-laden westerly winds, it is repainted every year with a coat of tar. The blackness of this toxic material immediately evokes the works the artist made here, as well as the Claude glasses used by 18th-century landscape painters to reduce the visual field to its main features.

Visiting the garden before entering the house, as one does when arriving at a friend's home, I noticed a poem by John Donne,[6] *The Sun Rising*, on the southern wall of the cottage, written in black letters cut into the timber. Black on black, I had not noticed it on Howard Sooley's photograph that fills the double-title page spread of *Derek Jarman's Garden*:[7]

Thou, sun, art half as happy as we,
In that the world's contracted thus;
Thine age asks ease, and since thy duties be
To warm the world, that's done in warming us.

By placing this text in front of everyone's gaze, Jarman shared his love of poetry. Literature, language and writing played a central role in his life and work.[8] This first visit to Prospect Cottage confirmed this for me.

Inside the house, it was clear to me that his office was just as important as his studio. His desk takes central position there, facing the window overlooking the garden. From the studio to the veranda at the back of the house, shelves run along the corridors to accommodate his collection of books, assembled there after his move from London. A visit to this 'library' reveals its owner's vast erudition, his curiosity about the past, myths and magic, as well as his connections to contemporary philosophy, art, cinema – Jean Cocteau and Pier Paolo Pasolini in particular – and Pop culture.

4 Gallerist Amanda Wilkinson represents Derek Jarman's pictorial oeuvre and is a member of the Keith Collins Will Trust. I would like to thank her for helping me to organise this exhibition.

5 Derek Jarman, *Derek Jarman's Garden* [1995], Thames & Hudson, London 2012.

6 John Donne (1572–1631), English poet and preacher, considered the leading exponent of metaphysical poetry.

7 Howard Sooley (b. 1963), artist and photographer, Derek Jarman's friend.

8 Derek Jarman wrote several books. The first was a book of poems, *A Finger in the Fishes Mouth* (1972), followed by *Dancing Ledge* (1984), and then the autobiography *Modern Nature* (1991). In 1992, he published *At Your Own Risk. A Saint's Testament*, and then *Chroma: A Book of Colour – June '93*, in 1994. Some of his books were published posthumously, such as *Smiling in Slow Motion*, written between 1991 and 1994 and published in 2000.

Outside wall of Prospect Cottage adorned with *The Sun Rising* (published in 1633) by John Donne, 2019

The art historian Robert Mills, author of studies on medieval homosexuality and a major book on the artist,[9] had been invited to exhibit part of Derek Jarman's library in the *Derek Jarman Protest!* exhibition organised in Dublin in 2019. In the catalogue, Mills indicates that he consulted this library on several occasions between 2014 and 2017.[10] An illuminating section of this prolific retrospective, it has informed my knowledge and analysis of Jarman's oeuvre, and, in a way, inspired the basis of the exhibition at Crédac. The exhibition was built around language, and it brought together series such as the *Black Paintings* (1986–1991) and the *Slogan Paintings* (1992–1993),[11] as well as the film *Blue* (1993), the artist's final opus. A selection from the series of assemblages (1986–1992) made at Dungeness was also on show. With their dimensions similar to reliquaries Jarman composed them from objects found on the beach, glass and broken mirrors encrusted in thick black oil paint or tar, also used to coat the canvas. Brambles, rusty nails, rosaries, keys, fragments of clothing, photographs, candles, compasses, knives, condoms, bullets – all objects with symbolic connotations. Engraved on glass, printed on plates, inscribed in the material itself, language is omnipresent, whether in the form of literary quotations, poems, slogans, philosophical aphorisms or newspaper headlines. His assemblages encapsulate significant data and details. Gold leaf, for example, has a sacred meaning. The objects he collected for his compositions were part of the vanitas motif. They would be used in turn by the artist to create his assemblages or to continue the gradual construction of his garden-mausoleum, where he created tiny monuments to departed beings.

All Jarman's works manifested his fierce desire to communicate – language is what is primarily confiscated from so-called marginal communities. As with Robert Rauschenberg (1925–2008) or Cy Twombly (1928–2011) – two artists he admired – words or dedications to literary loves are contained within the works, whether paintings, assemblages or films. Surfaces are covered with quotations, slogans, poems, philosophical aphorisms and insults.

A rich and eclectic collection of over 1,200 titles, it is not easy to sum up his book collection: books on art, architecture, gardening, history and religion coexist with works of poetry and psychology, annotated and commented on, often

9 Robert Mills, *Derek Jarman's Medieval Modern*, D.S. Brewer, Cambridge 2018.

10 Robert Mills, 'Derek Jarman's Library', in Seán Kissane (ed.), Seán Kissane and Karim Rehmani-White (eds.), *Derek Jarman Protest!*, Irish Museum of Modern Art/Thames & Hudson, Dublin/London 2020, p. 239–246. *Derek Jarman Protest!* exhibition was presented at the Irish Museum of Modern Art (IMMA), Dublin, 15 November 2019–23 February 2020; it then returned to the Manchester Art Gallery, Manchester, 2 December 2020–10 April 2021.

11 Also known as the *Queer Paintings* because they were produced by Derek Jarman for his exhibition entitled *Queer* at the Manchester City Art Gallery in 1992.

mentioning the date and place of their acquisition or the origin of a gift. It is a resource-library that nourished Jarman all his life.

In kinship with Robert Mills, I share here part of my enlightening visit to the Prospect Cottage library: William Shakespeare, Jean Genet, Truman Capote, William S. Burroughs and Allen Ginsberg's *Howl and Other Poems* (1956),[12] which Jarman bought on his first trip to the United States in 1964, in the iconic City Lights Bookstore in San Francisco. There are also Leonardo da Vinci's *A Treatise on Painting* (c. 1490), Leon Battista Alberti's *On Painting* (1435), Isaac Newton's *Opticks* (1704), Johann Wolfgang von Goethe's *Theory of Colours* (1810), Pliny the Elder and his *Natural History* (77), and Aristotle's *On Colours* (384–322 BC). Gardening manuals, including one by the great English landscape gardener Gertrude Jekyll (1843–1932), also populate the shelves and fed into his thinking.

A study of his library reveals the roots of his great passions and the founding subjects of his work, whether cinematographic, pictorial, literary or militant: alchemy, colour theory, herbalism, sexuality and queer theories. William H. Gass' *On Being Blue: A Philosophical Inquiry* (1976), for example, explores the significance of the colour blue as an emblem of mystery and cosmic depth. It is likely to have influenced Jarman in his formal experiments, and enabled him to conceive *Blue*.

Iconic, *Blue* is at once his last film, his last painting and his last text, closely linked to his book *Chroma: A Book of Colour*,[13] written a few months before his death. Each of the chapters in *Chroma* is devoted to the history, symbols and origins of a colour. The book traces the main elements between the consequences of his illness, his relationship with time and death, art and the colours he grew in his garden. The chapter devoted to the colour blue stands out from the others because it is largely dedicated to his experience of HIV. The film *Blue* also evokes the esoteric artist Yves Klein (1928–1962), the great master of colour who advocated the dematerialisation of painting. With *Blue*, the image is no more; it is a pared down sketch that touches on

Prospect Cottage, 2023

12 A book that reveals his enthusiasm for the poetry of the Beat Generation.
13 Derek Jarman, *Chroma: A Book of Colour – June '93*, Century, London 1994.

mysticism. The only thing that remains is the colour, which we stare at while the materiality of the body disappears. *Blue* is an invitation to listen: the diary of Jarman's illness and galloping blindness is read by several friendly voices, those of the actress Tilda Swinton, John Quentin and Nigel Terry – actors in several of his films – as well as his own voice, accompanied by sounds and music composed by his friend, the musician Simon Fisher Turner.

On the shelves of the library, meticulously arranged and catalogued by Keith Collins,[14] Jarman's final companion, are books by John Dee (1527–1608), an English mathematician, astronomer, astrologer, geographer and occultist, who devoted much of his life to the study of alchemy, divination and hermeticism. The title of the film *The Angelic Conversation* (1985) is borrowed from one of his opuses. Further on are Henri-Corneille Agrippa's *The Philosophy of Natural Magic* (1510) and Carl Gustav Jung's *Alchemical Studies* (1967), a work that reveals the Swiss psychoanalyst's interest in the philosophical, religious and psychoanalytical aspects of alchemy. Alchemy, in which Jarman had a deep interest, can be seen in some of his early Super-8 films – a form of cinema that the artist described as a marriage between light and matter – but also in his painting-assemblages, particularly in their relationship to transgression and metamorphosis. In a chapter of *Chroma* devoted to the colour silver, he notes: 'Mercury was sovereign of the metals, it was both silver and red, it was the mirror and path leading to the Conjunctio. It was seen as the primordial water, both guide and psychopomp. Since all metals shared a soul, it could lead the way to the conclusion of the task.'[15]

Research by Robert Mills reveals that Jarman also owned a copy of *The Herball* (1597) by the Elizabethan botanist John Gerard (1545–1612), which he quotes in *Modern Nature*. From it he drew a mixture of medicinal and folk references, as well as references to plants that he naturally introduced into the Dungeness garden, such as

14 Keith Collins (1964–2018) was a pivotal figure in Derek Jarman's life from the moment they met in 1987. He appeared in his films *The Garden* (1990), *Edward II* (1991) and *Wittgenstein* (1993) under his stage name, Kevin Collins.

15 Derek Jarman, *Chroma*, p. 76–77.

Prospect Cottage, 2019

borage, foxglove and marigold. Other volumes in his library include those by Vita Sackville-West (1892–1962), Virginia Woolf's companion and a member of the Bloomsbury Group, a reference for Derek Jarman for both her literary and gardening qualities; Christopher Marlowe's *Edward II* (1592); Michel Foucault's *History of Sexuality* (1976–1984), which Jarman bought in 1986 in its English translation, and which informed his views on sexuality, particularly in his later years when he adopted the term 'queer' as a vehicle for identity and protest.

He owned a copy of John Boswell's *Christianity, Social Tolerance and Homosexuality: Gay People in Western Europe, from the Beginning of the Christian Era to the Fourteenth Century* (1980), a pioneering book that helped to bring gay and lesbian history to the fore in the 1980s, and from which he derived a sense of sexual community throughout history. For the exhibition's showcases Mills also chose the book by visionary painter, poet and printmaker William Blake (1757–1812), *The Marriage of Heaven and Hell* (c. 1790), a copy of which Jarman owned. Lastly, although he was openly atheist, the Bible was in his library: we can assume that it also fertilised his imagination. The most annotated sections are the Book of Revelation and the Book of the Last Judgement, texts that influenced the apocalyptic imagery of the films *The Last of England* (1987), *The Garden* (1990) and *Blue*.

In his Super-8 films, Jarman's camera acts like a paintbrush. But in *Blue*, colour is all that remains. However, as Vanina Géré points out, *Blue* is 'not a manifesto against the formalist idea of pure colour, because in Jarman's work, colour is permanently connected to all aspects of life and the living, including memory and the imaginary; and if there is no pure colour, in the sense of unmixed colour, nor pure abstraction in the paintings-texts of the 1990s, it is perhaps also because purity has no place in a resolutely queer universe, which fights both artistically and ideologically against the stigmatisation of contaminated people'.[16]

Thus my first visit to Dungeness took me from the garden to the library, two places for putting down roots and leaving traces. The relationship between them is ancient and symbolically rich. Metaphorically, this relationship refers to an intelligence that develops a link between thought and action.

16 Vanina Géré, 'L'abstraction militante, Derek Jarman, dernières œuvres', *La Vie des idées*, Collège de France, Paris 2021, see https://laviedesidees.fr/L-abstraction-militante (last accessed September 2024).

These two microcosms are two miniature reconstructions of the universe into which Derek Jarman's intelligence and sensitivity were projected. The garden represents nature inhabited by humans, and the library brings together the constructions of the mind. It was at the crossroads of these two places that I forged my conviction that Jarman's great erudition built a continuum between culture and nature, society and the intimate. A kind of sophisticated compost from which an extremely cultivated visual work blossomed. Therefore, in putting together the exhibition at Crédac, I kept the active force of his language constantly in mind. Produced at a time when he was physically weak, the *Slogan Paintings* series expresses his anger and that of his contemporaries, for whom he is the megaphone. The trace of the struggle is inscribed in the material, at once fluid in movement and dense in content. With a fragile but determined hand, Jarman traced his enraged words in the very layer of paint that comes apart. In these works he combines unrestrained painting with militant signage. He reveals, as much as he erases, the homophobic and insulting press front covers that form the background of his paintings.

'Do I rebel against my situation? Yes, truly, and if you want to know, it scares me, and I think I rebel in a certain way, in my situation as an HIV-positive person... That's the particularity of our situation. It forces us to question ourselves, which I think is important. Perhaps my paintings are messages for those who see the black in them. They're almost like postcards. They're not grandiose, but they can have grandiose intentions.'[17]

This *Slogan Paintings* series was produced between two deaths: the loss of his sight, due to the consequences of HIV/AIDS, and his actual death, which occurred shortly after the paintings were completed. With Claude Monet (1840–1926), who he admired equally for two reasons, his painting and the creation of his garden,[18] Jarman shared blindness as a third commonality. Commenting on Monet, the painter Colette Brunschwig (b. 1927) noted: 'Anxiety seems to express not only the fear of threatening blindness, but also a kind of feverishness, an urgency to stabilise this erosion, this slow-motion rupture which, before his very eyes, will strike at even the most solid and defined forms.'[19] However, if for Monet the garden had become the subject of his painting, for Jarman it

17 In an exhibition catalogue of works by Derek Jarman for a retrospective of his films at the Accattone cinema, Paris 1989, p. 5.

18 Derek Jarman made his last trip to Giverny with Howard Sooley in May 1993 to visit Claude Monet's garden, where the French painter spent the last part of his life devoting himself to creating the *Water Lilies*.

19 Colette Brunschwig, 'Sur Claude Monet', written in 1960, published in 1999 in *Lignes* magazine, no. 37, p. 124–131.

was the site of a form of modern impressionism, that of the literary transcription of fleeting impressions, of the instability of things and the passing of the seasons. It was in their gardens that Monet and Jarman painted in the latter part of their lives. A garden is by its very nature unfinished, like *The Water Lilies* (1914–1926), the completion of which Monet constantly delayed. In the studio, Jarman wrote on the canvas; in the street, he was an activist. Creating and expressing himself were two forms that seemed to keep at bay the passage to nothingness that Jarman felt was imminent.

The layout of the exhibition *Dead Souls Whisper* at Crédac took the public from rooms presenting paintings and assemblages, accompanied by Super-8 films, to the *Blue* screening room. The aim of this exhibition design was to allow visitors to experience the gradual disappearance of the visual in favour of sound; a journey from the written word to the spoken word, in the voice of Derek Jarman, overwhelmed by progressive and encroaching blindness. In spite of everything, he delivered this very specific painting, depicting life and death, full of rage and anger. Jarman conceived his *Blue* film-confession for words, making himself accessible only through the faculties of language. Abstract, he floats in the mind and continues his oeuvre in the memory of the spectator.

Marco Martella has described Jarman's writing as 'poetry with fingernails black with earth'.[20] This is what we wanted to show in this, Jarman's first major exhibition in France, which went beyond the artist's genius to examine the role of the artist in society, and the use of art as a form of activism and testimony.

20 Teodor Ceric, preface by Marco Martella, *Jardins en temps de guerre*, Actes Sud, Arles 2014, p. 11.

Derek Jarman in Claude Monet's garden, Giverny, 1993

DEAD SOULS WHISPER (1986–1993)

LE CRÉDAC, 2021

PAGES 25–43: Exhibition views, *Derek Jarman. Dead Souls Whisper (1986–1993)*, Centre d'art contemporain d'Ivry – le Crédac, Ivry-sur-Seine, 2021

PUTRID
PUS

AIDS
BLOOD

HE CALLED IT LOVE BUT I CALL IT MURDER
LOVE
SEX

AIDS
BLOOD

Death is all things we see awake
All we see asleep is sleep

AIDS BLOOD IN M&S PIES' PLOT
18 VICE BOYS IN AIDS REVENGE

THE COLOURS OF DISGUST

ÉLISABETH LEBOVICI

Derek Jarman and his assistants, Richard Salmon studio, London, 1992

The painting looked to me like a bruised mass, scarred by words (see p. 83). In this aggregate of painting, with its ochre background more or less covered in layers of blood red turned brown, sullied by patches of green and furrows of electric blue, beaten by scrapings and cross-hatching, is written, in whitish capitals: PUTRID/FUCKUP/PUS/SCREWED BY/ THE CABINET. Evocative words, whose acrid connotations, inscribed upon the viscous matter, add to the sordidness of the citation. The latter comes from one of those tabloids that stank up and continue to stink up Great Britain – *The Sun*, for example, which provides this headline serving as a title for the painting: *Now we've ALL been screwed by the Cabinet.*[1] Here there is no pretty little foot, like the one that appeared under the 'wall of paint' out of which Honoré de Balzac had composed his *Unknown Masterpiece*, and which suggested 'a woman under there'.[2] There is no salvational figure in Derek Jarman, no foot by way of redemption. The undersurfaces of the painting make concrete the display of violence of the newspapers from 1980–1990. These made everyday targets of 'homos', mixed up in the panic of HIV/AIDS contamination, for which they were held responsible and therefore guilty. 'Britain Threatened by Gay Virus Plague' (*The Daily Mail*, 1985); 'I'd Shoot my Son if He Had AIDS, Says Vicar' (*The Sun*, 1986). Etc. In the series of *Queer Paintings* (1992–1993) that includes the work I have just described, Jarman used these headlines as backgrounds to his paintings. They repeat and repeat, photocopied and glued *all-over* and *ad libitum* on the structure, given over to the paint and the words that chisel and sometimes hammer them like old leather. Often, scarcely a few words stay afloat: 'Sick', 'Poofs', 'Dizzy Bitch'. Violence is topical. 'Even', is a surviving word from a series of terms forming or not a legible line: 'Sweet Queer 16 Soho Teenage AIDS Vice Boys Revenge Blood Spread the Even Plague' (*Spread the Plague*, 1992, p. 91). So that the paint accumulates 'on' and 'against' these disgusting backgrounds. Layers of strident colours join, intermix. What are we to call these colours? What name can be given to these red-blood/shit-brown, rotten-green/puss-yellow, blue-yuck that form the landscape of suffering,

1 *The Sun*, 17 September 1992.

2 Honoré de Balzac, *Le Chef-d'œuvre inconnu*, first published in 1831 (*The Unknown Masterpiece*, trans. Richard Howard, NYRB, New York 2001, p. 40–41): '"All I see are colours daubed one on top of the other and contained by a mass of strange lines forming a wall of paint" [...] Coming closer, they discerned in one corner of the canvas, the tip of a bare foot emerging from this chaos of colours, shapes and vague shadings, a kind of incoherent mist; but a delightful foot, a living foot! [...] "There's a woman under there," Porbus cried!'

Derek Jarman working with tar, c. 1991

of pain, of grief, of illness, of anger and of rage? Disgust and disgusting, here, truly are coloured and colouring sensations.[3] The *Queer Paintings* (which are followed by the *Evil Queen, Last Paintings* series [1993–1994] shown posthumously[4]) thus compose a riposte to the power of words, those that directly inscribe onto bodies the insult they carry; those words that produce abject bodies, rendered both repugnant and fascinating by the powers of horror.[5]

The disgusting as a political body. It is more or less this hypothesis that I would like to share in this text. It came to me as a raw reaction each time I visited one of Jarman's exhibitions.[6] Each time I encountered something unassimilable, unapprovable – something with which I did not feel 'at home' – expressed in the dull, massive, thick, greasy matter, and the shrill and glaring tints of certain paintings. Nevertheless, both disgust and homosexuality come into play, as the philosopher Martha C. Nussbaum, who devoted more than one work to these emotions that reject, humiliate, discriminate, has remarked. When they are confronted with homosexual acts and relations, she writes, some people feel 'a deep aversion akin to that inspired by bodily waste, slimy insects and spoiled food – and then cite that very reaction to justify a range of legal restrictions, from sodomy laws to bans on same-sex marriage'.[7] Disgusting, faggot: same struggle. It remains to be translated here, in these pages, to give you the aroma to inhale – a losing battle I think.

Not that disgust does not already have its place in art history: a sizable place, even. This emotion, which seems to be the most instinctive, is in fact one of the most creative. 'Disgust for all its visceralness turns out to be one of our more aggressive culture-creating passions', William Ian Miller recalls in *The Anatomy of Disgust*.[8] Georges Bataille made wide use of it. His philosophy of formlessness grants a transgressive power – and thereby a productive sacrament – to that downward motion (a 'low materialism'[9]) that functions like spitting. On the side of art history, the theory of the formless allowed for the identification of a way out of modern formalism. On the side of the artists, Cy Twombly (1928–2011) is probably one of its most plausible incarnations. In both of his essays on this American artist who lived exiled in Rome, Roland Barthes insists upon the both diabolically scatological and singularly

3 The expression 'colouring sensations' (*sensations colorantes*) is from Paul Cézanne.

4 The *Queer* exhibition took place at Manchester City Art Gallery in May–June 1992, before travelling to Rome and Potsdam. It was comprised of seven 'asphalt' paintings from 1989–1990, nine paintings exhibited in Glasgow earlier the same year and 28 paintings commissioned by the art centre, a large number of which were oversized (251,5 x 149/179 cm). *Evil Queen, Last Paintings* (*Evil Queen* from Walt Disney's *Snow White*) was held at Manchester's Whitworth Art Gallery in 1994. See Jeffrey Horsley, 'Queering the City: Manchester 1992', in Seán Kissane and Karim Rehmani-White (eds.), *Derek Jarman Protest!*, Irish Museum of Modern Art/Thames & Hudson, Dublin/London 2020, p. 212–235.

5 I am taking up Julia Kristeva's title, *Powers of Horror: An Essay on Abjection* (1980), trans. Leon S. Roudiez, Columbia University Press, New York 1982.

6 *Derek Jarman Protest!*, Irish Museum of Modern Art (IMMA), Dublin, 2019–2020; *Derek Jarman. Dead Souls Whisper (1986–1993)*, Le Crédac, Ivry-sur-Seine, 2021; Amanda Wilkinson Gallery, London, which represents the artist's estate.

7 Martha C. Nussbaum, *From Disgust to Humanity: Sexual Orientation & Constitutional Law*, Oxford University Press, Oxford 2010, p. 13.

8 William Ian Miller, 'Prologue', *The Anatomy of Disgust*, Harvard University Press, Cambridge 1997, p. 12.

9 See Rosalind Krauss and Yve-Alain Bois, *L'Informe: mode d'emploi*, exh. cat., Centre Pompidou, Paris 1996.

seasoned aftertaste that Twombly's work suggests.[10] He inventories several terms like claw, stain, macula, smear, which expose in broad daylight the impulsive experience carried by the traces of fingers, hands, graphite or colouring-crayon rubbings, coagulations and daubs of wax and oil paint, to say nothing of the adjunctions of semen or saliva – which Twombly is also reputed to have used on his canvases. All of which to orchestrate cultural inscriptions drawn from the refined register of classical knowledge, whose surnames the artist picks off, traced in jerky, gauche, trembling writing: Virgil, John Keats, Stéphane Mallarmé, Paul Valéry, Nicolas Poussin, the Marquis de Sade. Here, the disgusting is at the service of the sublime: a sublime that cauterises the effusions emerging from the artist's body, his impulses, his wounds, his sexuality, with a closet separating the private life of 'the man' and the public life of 'the work', in keeping with the patriarchal laws of modernity.

Jarman, on the contrary, is not in the closet. His works are profoundly anchored in the visibility of his sexual orientation: 'I knew I wanted to paint very early on – painting was my secret garden. My art was an escape out of Heterosoc.'[11] His sexual orientation – the adoption of the word *queer* would come later – situates him in a revolutionary perspective and a rejection of all assimilation (familial, religious, social...). And since 'most of our biography is situated in fiction',[12] Jarman utilises his life and his art for the purposes of political and social change; and this, as early as his engagement in 1970 at the heart of the Gay Liberation Front, and even further, after his seropositive diagnosis in 1986, which he made public in 1987. He was one of the first, if not *the* first, to do so in a Britain where homosexuality had been criminalised for so long, and which experienced, under Margaret Thatcher's iron rule, the resurgence of institutionalised homophobia using the HIV/AIDS epidemic as its pretext. In his first-person speech, delivered during the AIDS and Human Rights Conference in January 1988 in London, Jarman underscored his own serological status as much as the state obligation to change the course of repression in favour of education and support, as the organiser Peter Tatchell has chronicled. He was also a member of OutRage!, an activist organisation struggling for the repeal of Section 28 of the law on local government (introduced into

10 Roland Barthes, 'Cy Twombly : Works on Paper' (1979) and 'The Wisdom of Art' (1979), in *The Responsibility of Forms: Critical Essays on Music, Art, and Representation*, trans. Richard Howard, University of California Press, Berkeley and Los Angeles 1991, p. 157–176 and 177–194.

11 For Derek Jarman, 'Heterosoc' expresses the hegemony of heterosexual society: 'Heterosexuality isn't normal, it's just common', in *At Your Own Risk. A Saint's Testament*, University of Minnesota Press, Minneapolis 2010, p. 35.

12 Ibid., p. 82.

GBH Series II, 1983–1984

British law in 1988 and abolished in 2003). This law forbade 'the [intentional promotion] of homosexuality or publication of material with the intention of promoting homosexuality' and disallowed state schools from 'promot[ing] the teaching in any maintained school of the acceptability of homosexuality as a pretended family relationship'. Jarman was canonised during his lifetime, in 1991, in his Prospect Cottage garden, by the Sisters of Perpetual Indulgence, under the name Saint Derek of Dungeness of the Order of Celluloid Knights, 'in recognition of his films, books and everything he does for the gay and lesbian community and because he has a very sexy nose'[13] – which was not untrue.

The post-atomic look that reigns in the garden of Dungeness finds its extension in his reliquary paintings of vestiges, where garbage gleaned not far from there, on the coast of the English Channel, was thrown into hot tar: torn clothes, dried flowers, pieces of mirror or shards of glass, glasses, a toy aeroplane, white feathers, a crucifix, driftwood, barbed wire, rope, a broken boat in a bottle; even condoms and medication. The smothering usage of coal tar is in league with an epidemic history of painting and deformations, burns and blisters damaging the skin of painted surfaces. Largely used by artists of the first half of the 19th century such as Théodore Géricault, Eugène Delacroix and Gustave Courbet after Pierre-Paul Prud'hon, asphalt has in fact provoked a chemical reaction over time in the neighbouring colours, invading all of the layers without possible remedy. But as the use of disgust overturns the insult, the tar, which encompasses the objects with an oil slick, is also a conservation method for what was destined to disappear, what (and who) were thrown in the rubbish.

In the chapter 'Black Arts, O Mia anima nera' in *Chroma: A Book of Colour – June '93*, his alchemical manual of colours, Jarman wrote: 'Melanosis, moths which turn black to hide from predators.'[14] This is how he designates a pigmentation disorder and the phenomenon of 'industrial melanism'. It is a textbook case of natural selection: the transition towards a blackish colour operated by a species of moth, the peppered moth, in the central sites of the industrial revolution in Great Britain. The colour of the moths did in fact adapt to the colour of the birch trees and their lichens blackened by the soot of the

13 Ibid., p. 117–118.

14 Derek Jarman, *Chroma: A Book of Colour – June '93*, Century, London 1994.

GBH Series I, 1983–1984

coal used in manufacturing. The moths became black, more difficult for their bird and bat predators to identify. What Jarman does with his unquenchable erudition is not what Twombly does with his dedications ('To Valéry'; 'To Tatlin'), tendered to those he admires. In a single signifying chain Jarman links the personal, the artistic, the social and the cultural. 'One day', he wrote, 'the paintings will be seen as more than tantrums and will seem to be wet with my tears.'[15] It cannot be forgotten that the HIV/AIDS epidemic also affected those dying all around. It is by the alchemy of painting, in its troubling and striking materiality, that personal suffering interacts with collective and public sorrow. Jarman recounts his 'terrible state of agitation'[16] when he encountered the crucified Christ that Matthias Grünewald painted for the *Isenheim Altarpiece* (1516) for the Monastery of Saint Anthony (Isenheim), today preserved at the Unterlinden Museum at Colmar. The poor flayed body of the crucified is constellated with pestilential wounds and lesions. As for the figure of Saint Anthony, the patron saint of the monastery also represented in the altarpiece, it is covered in puffiness and abscesses. The fear and disgust inspired by the Black Plague is not very far: the epidemic of 1347–1352 brought about the disappearance of a huge part of the European world and its successive reappearances reverberated between the 14th and 16th centuries, constituting a permanent ground for horror for individuals threatened with collective death, for which Matthias Grünewald assumed the role of subject and chronicler.

'WHEN I WAS YOUNG, THE ABSENCE OF THE PAST WAS A TERROR. That's why I wrote an autobiography.'[17] Jarman's unbridled enlightenment can thus be understood as a search for a past to follow and to pursue between the lines of normative 'heterosoc' reading – activating a profoundly anachronistic, anti-linear, a-chronological history. And queer.[18] The film *Sebastiane* (1976), spoken wholly in Latin, rests entirely on the frenzied homoeroticism of renascent versions of the martyr. *Jubilee* (1978), his first punk film, brings Queen Elizabeth I back into the disenchanted landscape of the England of the late 1970s. The adaptation of Shakespeare's *The Tempest* (1979) continues with the matching of the bard's sonnets with grainy images of modern young people embracing (*The Angelic*

15 Derek Jarman, *Smiling in Slow Motion: Journals, 1991–1994* [2000], Vintage Classics, London 2018, p. 303.
16 Derek Jarman quoted by Robert Mills, *Derek Jarman Medieval Modern*, D.S. Brewer, Cambridge 2018, p. 49.
17 Derek Jarman, *At Your Own Risk*, p. 65.
18 See Robert Mills, p. 11.

Conversation, 1985), and plays, similarly, on this past that takes place in the present, and reciprocally. There is the same mixture of temporalities with his *Caravaggio* (1986). According to Jarman, the latter is subject to a 'mediaeval' approach whereas chronological norms situate the painter much later.[19] In 1991, Christopher Marlowe's play *Edward II*, was transformed into a film that castigates the religious repression of sexuality in the Middle Ages, and which, as in a game of billiards, collides with Jarman's own childhood and the days of HIV/AIDS. The screenplay connected to the film, entitled *Queer Edward II*, which combines the medieval hero and the activism of OutRage!, makes things even clearer. Several paintings from the *Queer Paintings* series (1992–1993) ally the repression of homosexuality and that of occidental culture. For example, *EIIR*, the Queen's monogram (Elizabeth II Regina), collapsed into the burning news of an issue of *People* magazine – 'SEX BOYS FOR SALE AT QUEEN'S GROCER' – covered in a lava of red and black paint upon which are scribbled the words *cocks* and *arse*, making use of the crudeness of the era of Elizabeth I (see *EIIR*, 1992, p. 77).

As with Twombly, Jarman's paintings invoke names. But for the latter, the incision of words or slogans into the humid matter stems much more from a will to *out* those words, just as he made public his HIV-positive status. Here we find the tactics of militant affirmation, where parody and the most derisory and most monstruous humour are carried at arm's length, as is the case constantly in the processions of ACT UP, OutRage! and, today, of #MeToo. Thus the opportunistic diseases and the damage they do are part of the dance: 'TB or not TB' (Tuberculosis + Hamlet monologue); 'Fuck Me Blind' (Screw me blindly + fuck me whereas toxoplasmosis has made me go blind); 'Blind Fail' (ditto + You failure!), 'Ataxia-AIDS is Fun' (associating a neurological ailment affecting one's equilibrium and coordination to the dark humour of the situation). I think also of 'AIDS is disco' from Act Up-Paris. Not to mention 'Dead Sexy' (sexy to death and dead sexy). It is also a way of saying that HIV/AIDS has no meaning, that the 'AIDS crisis is ridiculous',[20] that the virus does not mean anything. It is important to counteract the discourse from the far-right that sees in HIV a divine punishment or the revenge of a natural religious law, with nonsense.

19 See Robert Mills, p. 28ff. Caravaggio was active between 1592 and 1610.

20 Gregg Bordowitz, *The AIDS Crisis Is Ridiculous and Other Writi(1928-1987) ngs, 1986–2003*, MIT Press, Cambridge, Massachusetts 2004.

Thus, wrote the critic Stuart Morgan, Jarman's paintings propose 'a confrontation with surfaces which resembled painting, but which instead were engaged on a double errand, offsetting one type of communication with another, matching one mode of reading – word for word – with what might be considered its polar extreme, interpretation'.[21] It is not insignificant, then, that these traces are inscribed on a background prepared by the offensive everyday landscape displayed in kiosks and on the street: newspaper. It is a technique Jarman practised as early as 1983 for six large paintings entitled *GBH* (for Grievous Bodily Harm) – a circle painted over layers of newspaper, just as the Heresford *Mappa Mundi* was painted on a layer of parchment around 1300. The technique of newspapers as background support recalls not only Andy Warhol's (1928–1987) use of headlines, but also the silk-screened news excerpts on canvases by Robert Rauschenberg (1925–2008) – one of Twombly's early companions and an artistic model for Jarman. Or Nancy Spero (1926–2009), who never used 'raw' paint, but worked from printed, cut and glued figures. This work of layering in the paintings can be compared in particular to that which operates in Jarman's Super-8 films, which use and reuse images in the same manner, so that they also lose all causal relation, like those that govern traditional narrative film. Instead, they become textures.

21 Stuart Morgan, 'Borrowed Time', in Roger Wollen (ed.), *Derek Jarman. A Portrait*, Thames & Hudson, London 1996, p. 115.

22 In *Evil Queen. Last Paintings*, exh. cat., Whitworth Art Gallery, with Richard Salmon Ltd, Manchester 1994, p. 12–14.

The last pictorial series, *Evil Queen, Last Paintings* had nonetheless had enough of the gutter press. Has the latter mellowed? Is it not rather that the artist was finished with that version of time comparable to a stock exchange of news? In addition, his sight was increasingly fading. He could no longer read the defamatory newspaper titles, whereas the desire to confront, to interfere with, to mix with painting, as a corporeal and physical act, was ever stronger. Two assistants prepared the canvas, then Jarman, or the assistants if he was no longer able – and in that case he directed from a distance – would apply the paint in different thicknesses, sometimes slinging it like mud, using their hands to sink into it or make deep marks of the words that howl: 'Scream', 'Infection', 'Ouch (Arse Bandit)', crossing the painting out at its midriff and reading it like a death sentence ('Death'). 'The actual physicality of painting will release the violence in me.'[22] The matter manifests to the finger – or else to the eye – as carelessness, the visual result of which is of little importance. To find such a physical implication, I think it is necessary to look towards disarmed bodies, as Elsa Dorlin demonstrates: all those people who experience gender, race, class violence, who she invites to practise self-defence.[23]

I think, for example of Ana Mendieta (1948–1985), a Cuban artist exiled in the United States, and of the implication of her body, connected to exile as much through pain as through a possible resistance: 'Pain of Cuba, body I am.'[24] Wanting to commune with the earth, imprint her silhouette onto a landscape and leave a hollow trace of her passage. As many actions that create an alternation in which the body marks a place, while reactivating, as soon as it is no longer there, the pain of being torn from that same place: such is the series of *Siluetas* (1973–1980).

In April 1982, in New York's alternative space, the Franklin Furnace, Mendieta reactivated the *Body Tracks (Rastros Corporales)* performance she had already presented in November 1974, to the sound of beating drums, Afro-Cuban resurgences. Mendieta moved towards a wall upon which pieces of paper were glued, and before which was a bowl of animal blood and tempura paint set upon the ground. Immersing and coating her hands and her arms in the mixture, she approached the first piece of paper and firmly applied her hands and her arms on its surface. Then she moved towards the ground, and gradually the marks of her fingers traversed the traces left by the arms and the hands before them, so that a permanent work of representation and superimpositions of traces is visible, emphasised as she repeated this bloody gesture twice more before turning around and leaving the room. What interests me, both in this application and in its repetition, is that she exceeded the visual, that distance by which the artist is supposed to 'measure' her work, and become a means by which to enter into the landscape, an art of gardening, where time, as Jarman recalls, is 'without past or future, beginning or end'.[25]

But I should stop here. Because as I write, the disgust weakens and drains away...

23 Elsa Dorlin, *Se défendre. Une philosophie de la violence*, La Découverte, Paris 2017.
24 Nancy Spero (1926-2009), 'Tracing Ana Mendieta', *Artforum*, vol. 30, no. 8, April 1992, p. 75.
25 Derek Jarman, *Modern Nature: The Journals of Derek Jarman*, Century, London 1991, p. 30.

Canonisation of Derek Jarman as Saint Derek of Dungeness by the Sisters of Perpetual Indulgence, Prospect Cottage, September 1991

QUEER

MANCHESTER CITY ART GALLERY, 1992

PAGES 59–65: Exhibition views, *Queer*, Manchester City Art Gallery, Manchester, 1992

QUEER DEREK JARMAN
GEORGE
Telephone
Telephone

FILTH

FILTH
FILTH

QUEER (1992) AND *PROTEST!* (2021)

FIONA CORRIDAN

Derek Jarman, 1992

I'd been aware of Derek Jarman since I was a teenager growing up in Manchester in the late 1980s. He was one of the few public figures to talk about his HIV status, was publicly advocating for gay rights and rallying against Section 28 (the law passed in 1988 by the Conservative government that stopped councils and schools 'promoting the teaching of the acceptability of homosexuality as a pretended family relationship'). At a time when I was becoming more politically aware, Jarman made a huge impression on me. In television and radio interviews he sounded 'British establishment', but most certainly wasn't, and I was struck by his articulate and nuanced arguments delivered without condescension.

My first real experience of Jarman's art came in 1992, when Manchester City Art Gallery (as it was then called) worked with him to create his first solo exhibition in the city. By then I was thinking about applying to university and was recognising real shifts in the city I'd grown up in – a much more cosmopolitan culture was emerging. The Gay Village was developing and becoming a destination for people looking for an alternative to the traditional bar and club scene. I recognised that the gay scene was one where high and low culture blended quite happily. Pop music and fashion were equally celebrated alongside both traditional and avant-garde theatre, film and art, a space where anything goes, that felt very inclusive, even to someone who wasn't part of that community.

That said, I did still feel a sense of shock when I saw the banner *Queer Derek Jarman* on the 19th-century Athenaeum, the civic building that housed Manchester Art Gallery's exhibition programme. As a young straight woman, I wasn't aware of contemporary discourse among the gay community around terminology, and I had only experienced the word 'queer' being used in a derogatory way by bigots. *Queer Derek Jarman* changed that perspective. It was my first encounter with language being reclaimed and reused by a community in a positive way. The exhibition itself provided a different kind of shock, an assault on the senses through an explosion of colour, scale, emotion and language. Monumental, brightly coloured paintings obscured tabloid newspaper headlines, sacred and ephemeral objects were literally pushed into paint and tar, wordplay and slurs were etched or scrawled onto the surface of artworks. Jarman was using his gift for impassioned and articulate expression in a completely different way. That blend of high and low culture, the dualities of anger/humour; hate/love; sacred/profane and hypocrisy/authenticity leapt from the walls and into my consciousness. I have never shaken off that initial feeling of shock, or indeed wanted to.

Almost 30 years on and I was lucky enough to be part of a group of people who brought Jarman's work back to Manchester for the exhibition *Derek Jarman Protest!*. I was keen to recapture some of the emotion I had experienced in *Queer Derek Jarman*. In developing the Manchester exhibition, my co-curator Jon Savage and I wanted to harness and express something of the spirit of Jarman. This included his contradictions – his interest in tradition, classicism, religion, romanticism, myth and magic, along with his avant-garde approach, atheism, activism and strong connections to pop culture. The exhibition was broadly chronological. It followed his trajectory from art student to established painter, set designer and film-maker to music video maker, activist, writer and gardener. We aimed to present Jarman's many ways of working as a continuous flow; to consider how one practice informed another, how he fused his knowledge of tradition, myth and magic with new forms of expression and storytelling. Jarman's methods and use of media perfectly exposed and expressed the contradictions at the heart of society, the divisive politics and the savage realities of 1980s and 1990s Britain.

The retrospective depth of *Derek Jarman Protest!* shed light on his connection to modern British painting. Many of the artists he admired or felt an affinity with are represented in our collection at Manchester Art Gallery, including Wyndham Lewis (1882–1957), Paul Nash (1889–1946) and Keith Vaughan (1912–1977). Jarman's early experimentations in painting were directly influenced by some of these artists, and it was a revelation to discover one of his earliest paintings, *Self Portrait (After Wyndham Lewis)*

Wyndham Lewis, *Portrait of the Artist as the Painter Raphael*, 1921
Derek Jarman, *Self-Portrait (After Wyndham Lewis)*, 1959

(1959), a homage to our own Wyndham Lewis *Portrait of the Artist as the Painter Raphael* (1921). He also admired the Neo-Romantic artists of the first half of the 20th century, with their romantic veneration of Britain's past, and presentation of a supernatural, idealistic or even prophetic sense of the British landscape. Jarman's 1970s geometric landscapes (as well as his early Super-8 film *Journey to Avebury*, 1973) feature the Neolithic stones at Avebury in Southwest England, also a site of great importance to Paul Nash. The stark, barren landscape, use of geometric shapes and inclusion of monoliths in Jarman's *Avebury* series (1973) call to mind Nash's surreal *Nocturnal Landscape* (1938), also in our collection. These Neo-Romantic and Surrealist qualities are also evident in Jarman's later landscapes and assemblages featuring objects collected from the 'alchemical landscape' of Dungeness.[1]

Until recently, the only Jarman painting that Manchester Art Gallery owned was the titular painting from the 1992 *Queer* exhibition (see p. 95). We were keen to build on the success of *Derek Jarman Protest!* and develop the legacy further. We have recently acquired two works from Jarman's series of *Black Paintings* (1986–1991), which were conceived after he received his AIDS diagnosis in 1986. The *Black Paintings* have been described as 'small universes of anger, pain and sanctity'[2] and hold as much power today as they did over 35 years ago. We chose two of these works to acquire, which not only reference the political and social divisions exposed and articulated so powerfully by Jarman in the 1980s, but also speak to contemporary urgencies and debates around sexuality, national identity and societal divisions in 21st-century Britain.

British Scum (1987), though spare in terms of the aesthetic, is incredibly powerful, particularly in the context of the history of HIV/AIDS and LGBTQIA+ history in the UK. The rectangular piece of glass in the centre, with the beautifully engraved text in Jarman's own hand, can be seen as a reference to the UK government's 1980s public information campaign 'AIDS – Don't Die of Ignorance'. The TV advertisement and print

1 Jonny Bruce, 'The Alchemical Landscape of Dungeness', in Seán Kissane & Karim Rehmani-White (eds.), *Derek Jarman Protest!*, Irish Museum of Modern Art/Thames & Hudson, Dublin/London 2020, p. 261–266.

2 Pontus Kyander, introduction to the exhibition *Derek Jarman: Black Paintings* at Trondheim Kunstmuseum, Norway, 2014.

Paul Nash, *Nocturnal Landscape*, 1938
Derek Jarman, *Avebury Series no. 4*, 1973

publicity featured a black monolith or gigantic tombstone and served to panic rather than educate the population, promoting a culture of fear rather than understanding. Two discs set into the thick black paint have the appearance of a set of eyes peering out of the canvas, referencing the tradition of placing coins on the eyes of a corpse and, more personally, 'alludes to the terrible premonition of blindness that Jarman had to reconcile with as his illness progressively worsened'.[3]

This work will hold particular resonance for people living in and around Manchester in that period. The title and the etched text refer to James Anderton (1932–2022), the former Chief Constable of Greater Manchester. In 1986 – the height of the HIV/AIDS crisis – at a police training event, Anderton was quoted as saying that people living with AIDS were 'swirling in a human cesspit of their own making'. He had also once suggested that homosexuality be outlawed. He was heavily influenced by his faith and claimed he was 'channelling' God to speak out on moral issues. In Anderton's obituary in *The Guardian* Duncan Campbell wrote: 'Anderton made it clear that he felt answerable to a higher authority than the Home Office. "God works in mysterious ways", he said. "Given my love of God and my belief in God and Jesus Christ, I have to accept that I may well be used by God."'[4]

Jarman responded to Anderton's pronouncements by creating this visceral work. Its witty but scathing text, etched into the glass plate at the centre, lampoons the Chief Constable's communing with God claim. It reads:

MOVING IN MYSTERIOUS WAYS
Dear Jesus
who is the angel to
throw James Anderton
in the cesspit? give
us a break, ask
dad to strike him with
a thunderbolt or
better turn him into
a pillar of salt
Derek.
MODERN TIMES 1987

3 Matthew Cheale, 'Derek Jarman: painting, protest and the AIDS pandemic', Art UK, 2021, https://artuk.org/discover/stories/derek-jarman-painting-protest-and-the-aids-pandemic (last accessed September 2024).

4 Duncan Campbell, *Sir James Anderton Obituary* in *The Guardian*, 6 May 2022, www.theguardian.com/uk-news/2022/may/06/sir-james-anderton-obituary (last accessed September 2024).

Here Jarman satirises Anderton's 'moving in mysterious ways' comment and is channelling his own connection with Jesus, asking him to speak to God/'dad' and, drawing on the story of the tale of Sodom and Gomorrah from Genesis 19, turn Anderton 'into a pillar of salt'.

Anderton was a very divisive figure both in the city and nationally. At the time there were calls for him to resign over the comments he made. Despite his controversial views, he was allowed to stay in post and was knighted in 1990 before enjoying a full retirement, dying just in 2022. Members of the LGBTQIA+ community in the city still reference the former Chief Constable's comments when talking about the history of their community, how his public statements, regressive policies and the fear and division that they engendered are still keenly felt. In fact, the punk poet of colour Jay Mitra (b. 2000), in a piece written and performed for the Manchester Pride Candlelit Vigil in 2022, used the words 'Sex treated like a sin... When a Chief Constable snarled the word "cesspit".'[5] Though there is a great deal more tolerance and acceptance now, there is still a lot to unpick in terms of this history, and to address in terms of current prejudices faced by the LGBTQIA+ community.

The second *Black Painting* we have acquired is from *The Last of England* body of works. *Grievous Bodily Harm* (1986) was created while Jarman was working on his film *The Last of England*, released in 1987 (which had as a working title *GBH*). This work connects to a series of six important large-scale paintings that were shown as an installation at the ICA in London in 1984, and that formed part of a powerful installation at Void in Derry, Northern Ireland, in 2019. Two of the original six GBH paintings were shown in *Protest!*. At 3 metres high, and made of linen and newspaper covered in glue and thick impasto paint, they are incredibly vulnerable (see p. 50, 52). This smaller-scale painting from 1986 features the same imagery as the larger installation pieces. Emerging from under the thick layers of black paint is an outline of part of Britain rendered in fiery or blood-red paint as if burning. The edges are gold leaf, and embedded into the surface is a piece of shattered glass etched with words that often appear in Jarman's

5 Jay Mitra, *This Quilted History*, written in collaboration with the George House Trust (GHT) for Manchester Pride 2022. The poem is based on the archival material at GHT, interviews with those living with HIV, and the stories and photographs of those who have died.

British Scum, 1987

work from this period: *GB(H)*, *Night Life* and *Victorian Values*. These can be seen to reference, respectively: Great Britain and the political and social harm Jarman saw being inflicted on his country; darkness and the shadowy world imposed on the gay community connected to cruising and underground clubs; the hypocritical value system and laissez-faire economic policies that the conservative government, specifically Margaret Thatcher, wanted Britain to return to. This series critiqued what Jarman saw as the introduction of regressive and punitive policies and practices, such as Section 28, the dismantling of traditional industries and unfair economic policies that exacerbated inequalities in British society.

In this age of post-Brexit Britain, on-going economic crises and polarised debate around identity and sexuality, societal divisions have been exacerbated and made more visible. Once again, certain sectors of the population look to blame and attack those on the margins. Jarman's work continues to be relevant, and *Protest!* introduced a new generation to his work. We know from comments made by the public and younger LGBTQIA+ artists how important the exhibition was to them. Numerous people, including the performance artist David Hoyle (who was canonised in the exhibition by the Manchester Chapter of the Sisters of Perpetual Indulgence), told us that the exhibition made them feel 'accepted' in the city. It also led to a series of collaborative workshops with arts agency Short Supply, the creation of a new body of work by the artist-in-residence Jez Dolan and performances by Jade Blackstock and Shrek 666 as part of the radical festival Submerge.[6]

Derek Jarman's paintings, along with other recent acquisitions by previously marginalised or under-represented artists, will help us to introduce new voices to Manchester Art Gallery's collections, and support our focus on social justice. These artworks will be key in helping us to reflect on protest and activism in the past and present. They will be used at the Gallery as part of our work with communities to interrogate where power lies. They will help us to ignite debate about the role of the artist in society, and the creation and use of art as an alternative form of expression to promote positive social change.

6 Jez Dolan (b. 1966) is a British artist living and working in Manchester. His practice underlines the intersections between queerness, sexuality, identity and memory. In 2021–2022 he was artist in residence at Manchester Art Gallery during *Derek Jarman Protest!*. Jade Blackstock (b. 1993) is a British performance artist. Through her work she looks at Black ancestral traditions, myths and materialities that articulate and interrogate ongoing colonial systems, and manifest and develop within Black diasporic contexts. Shrek 666 is an ongoing project and ogre embodiment by Dæmon Clelland, a multidisciplinary Scottish artist and maker working within Live Art, special FX prosthetics, moving image, sound, radio, visual art and tattooing.

Grievous Bodily Harm, 1986

PAINTINGS 1991–1993

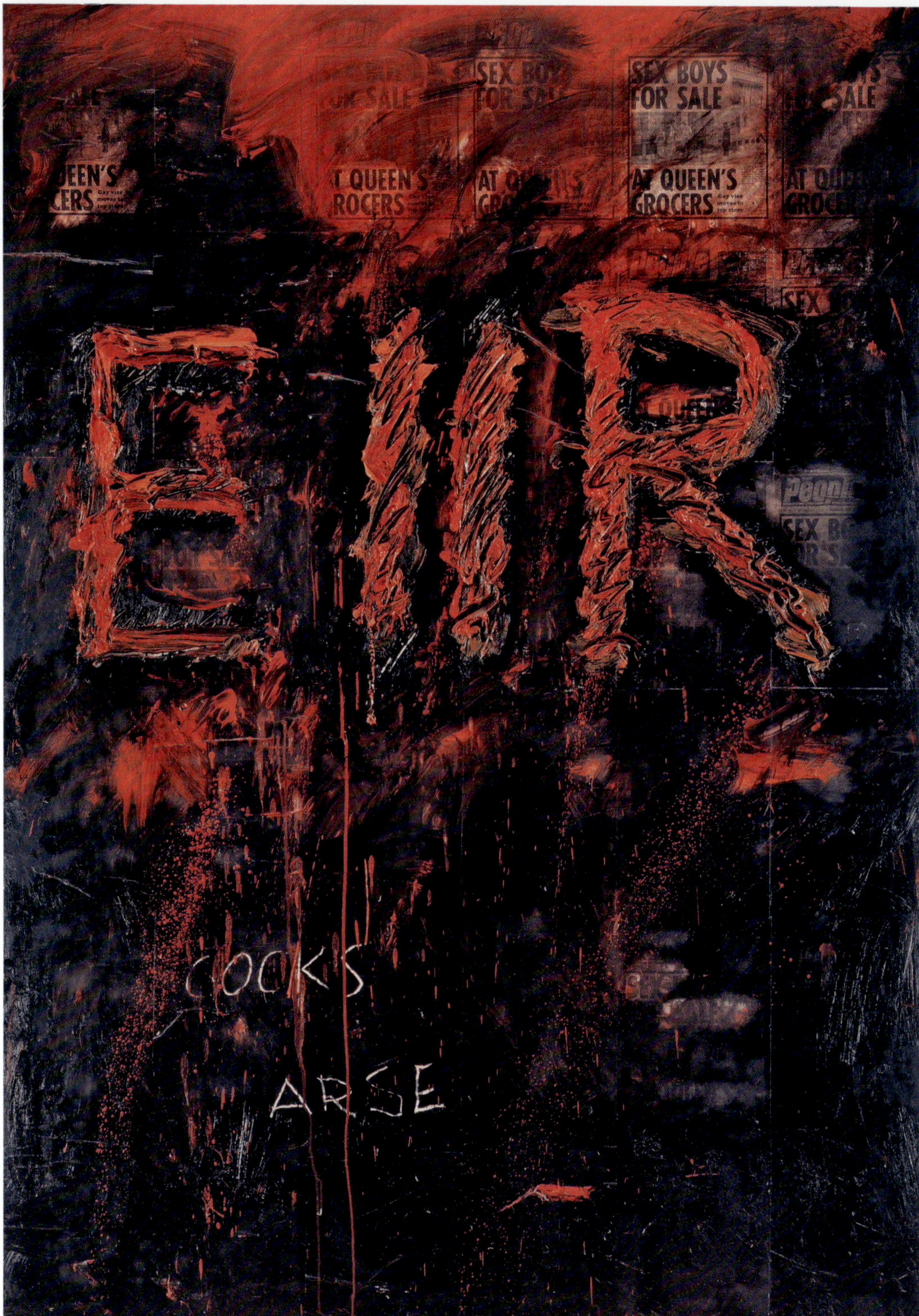

EIIR, 1992

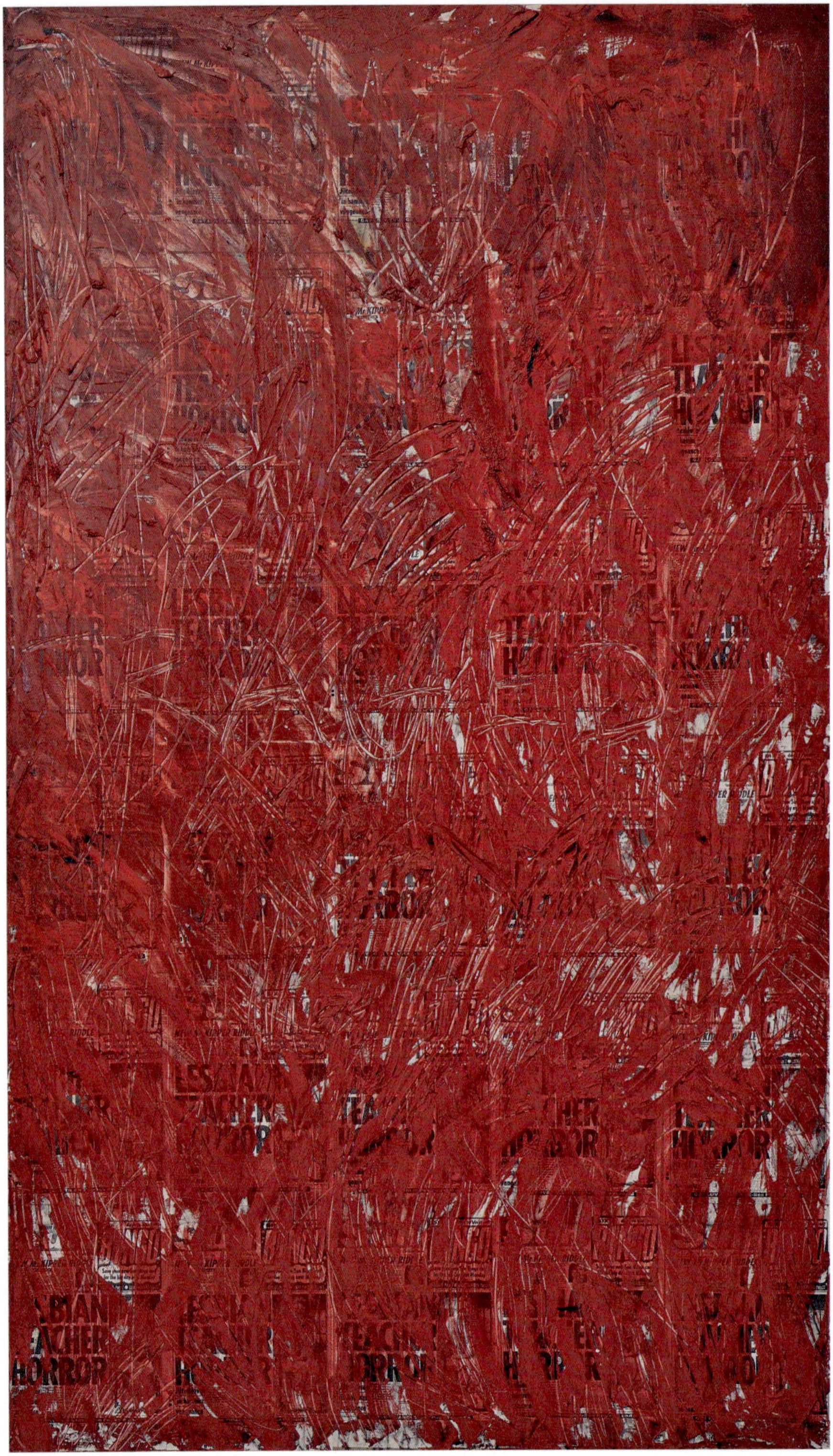

Tragedy, 1992

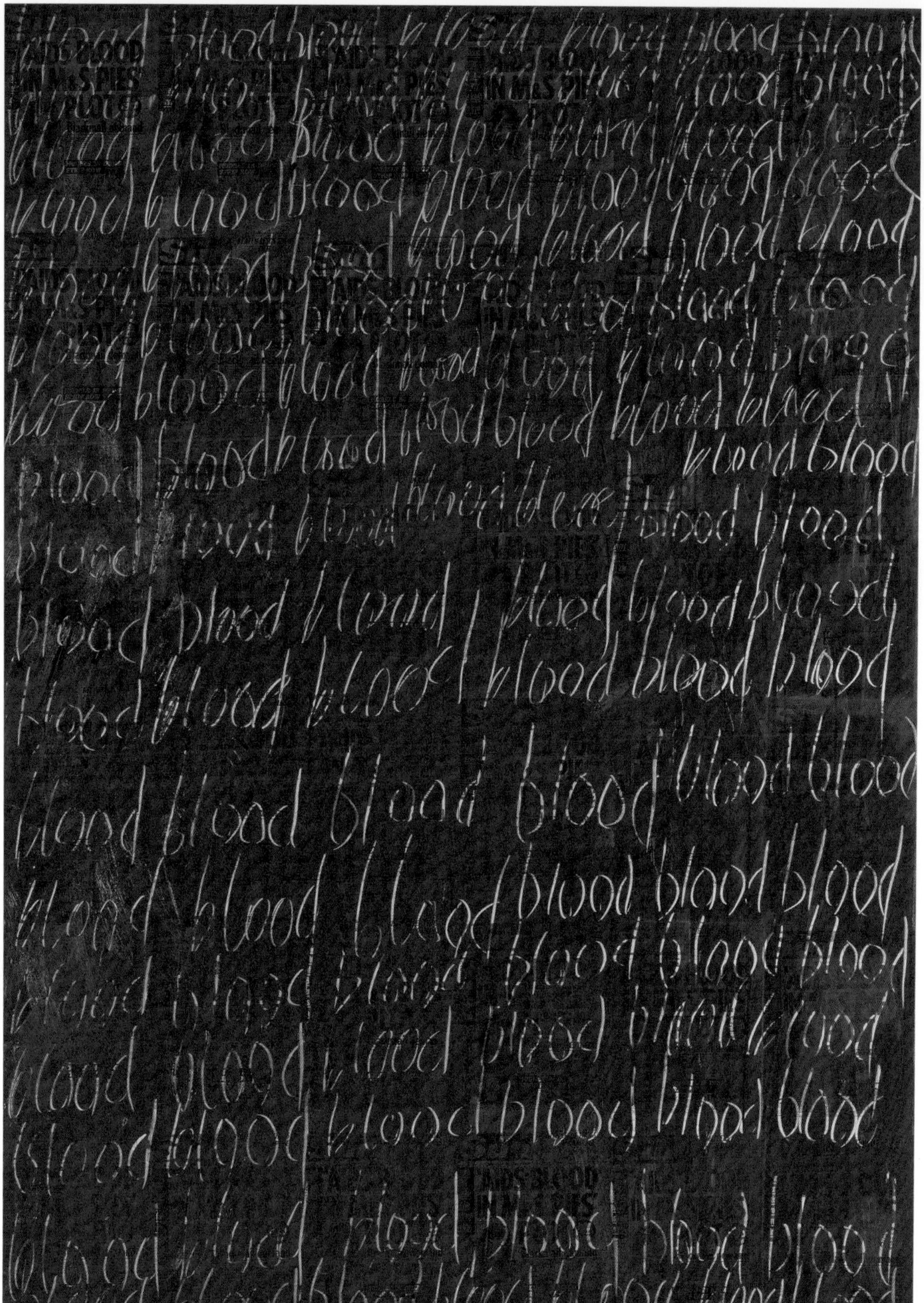

Blood, 1992

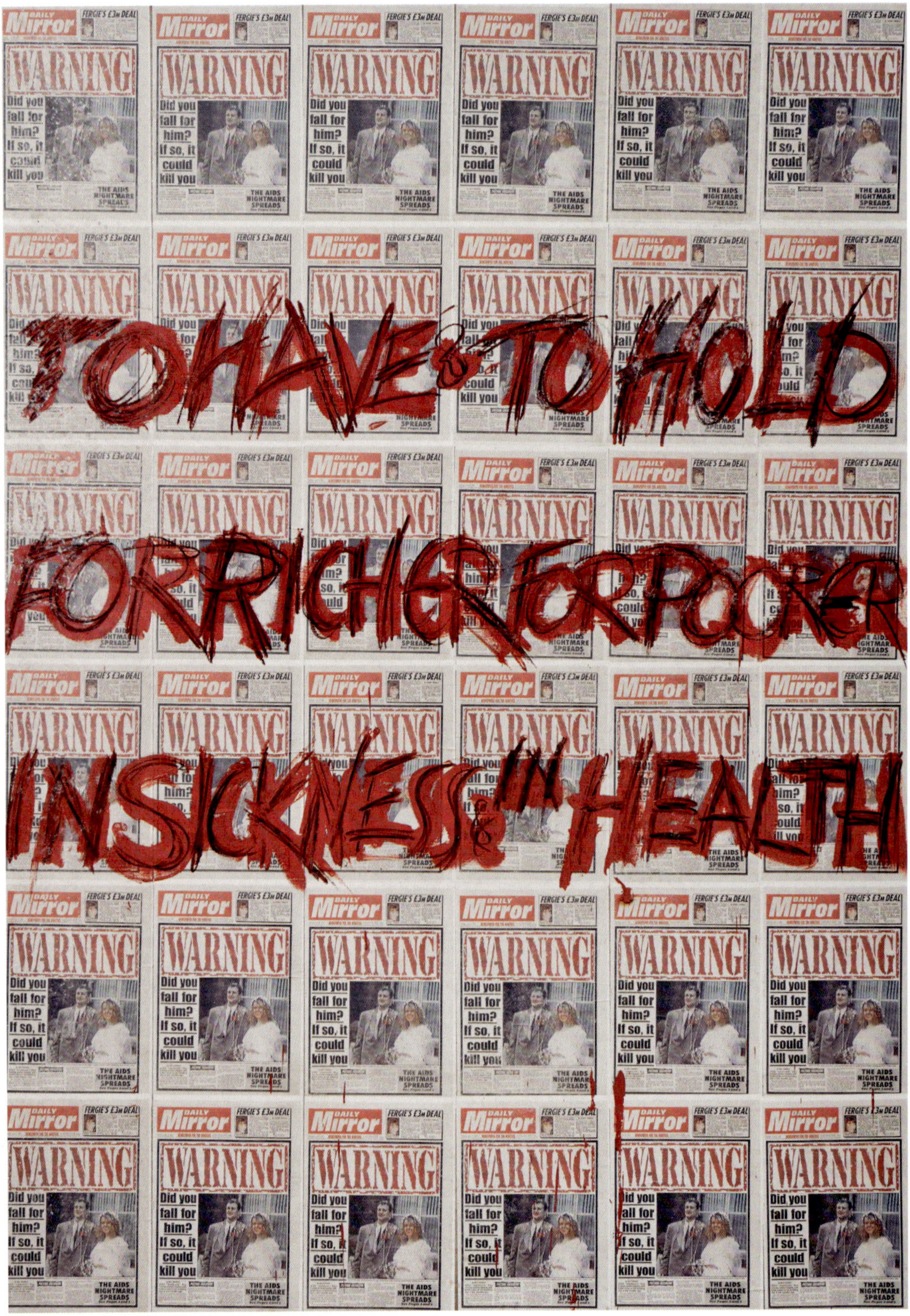

To Have and To Hold, 1992

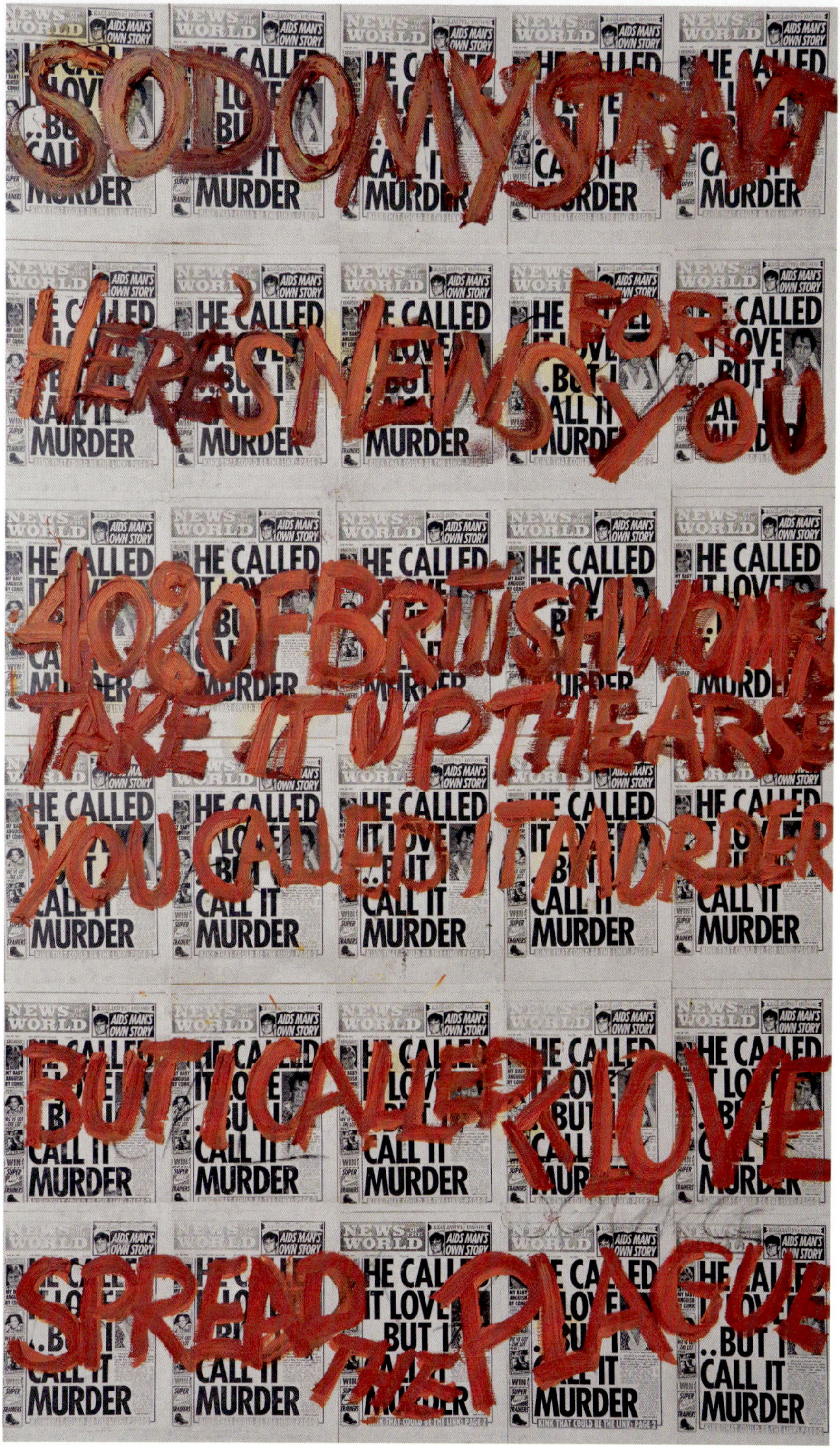

40% of British Women, 1992

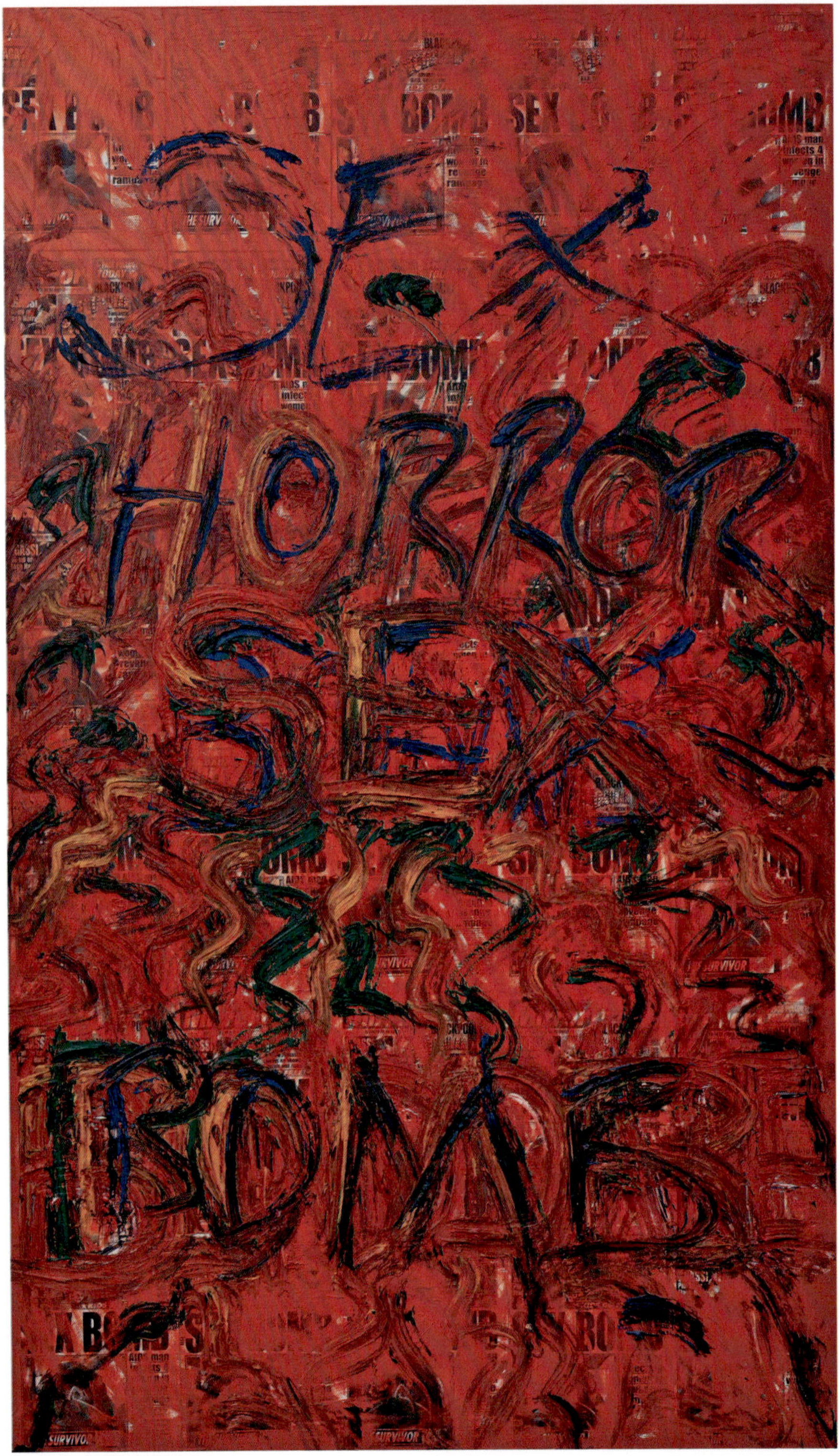

Blind Date, 1992

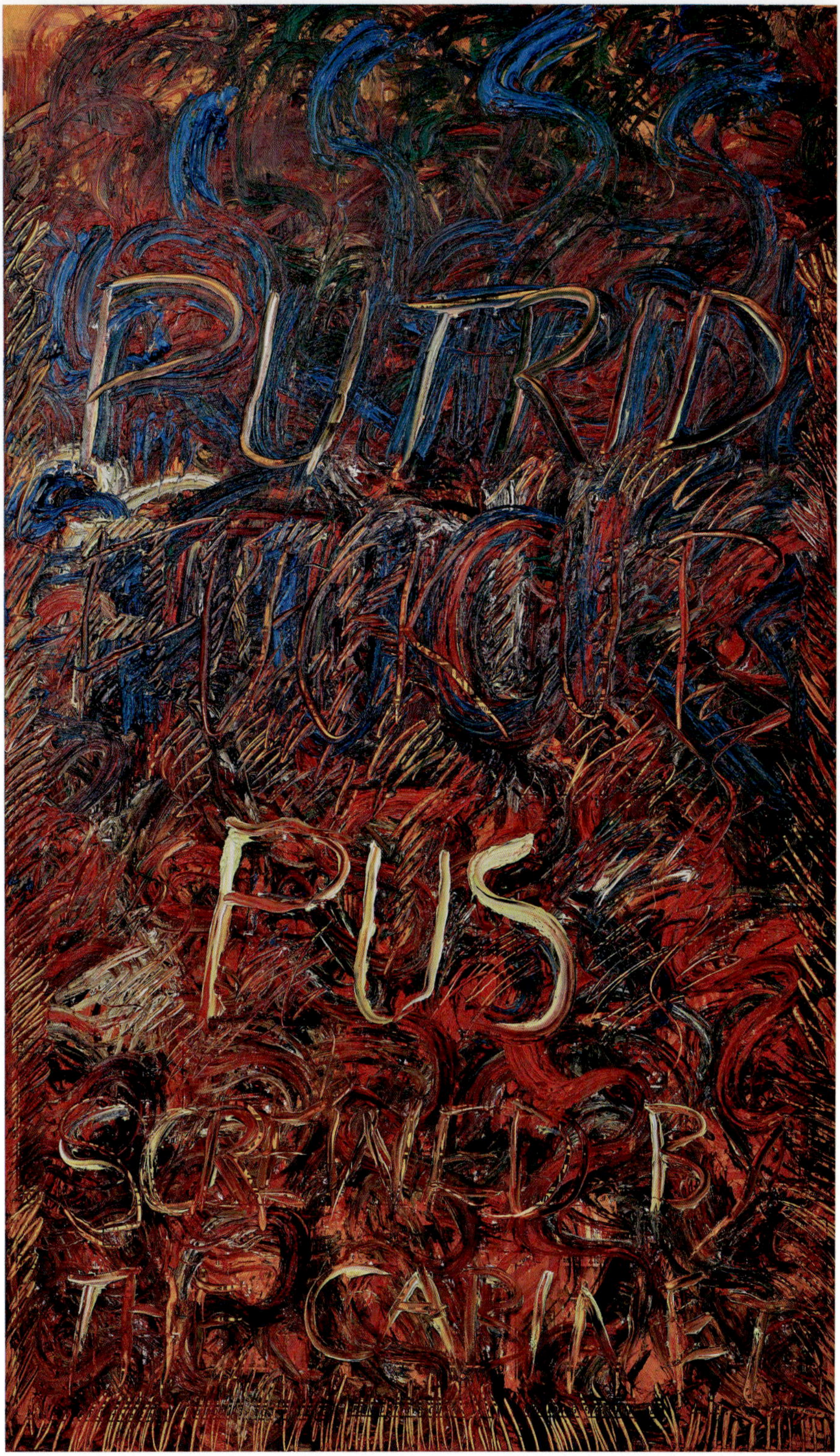

Now We've All Been Screwed by the Cabinet, 1992

Sun
PRINT STRIKE LEADER JAILED
GAY SANTA GETS SACK
Fairy grotto bust-up
WANTED: A FELLA FOR SEXY MARIA
TIME
dear Santa please send
ME

Time, 1992

SEX BOYS
COCKS AND ARSES
FOR SALE
AT QUEEN'S GROCERS
Gay vice moves to top store
FOR SALE
AT QUEEN'

Sold Out, 1992

Dead Angels, 1992

Negative Image, 1992

Spread the Plague, 1992

Letter to the Minister, 1992

Priest, 1992

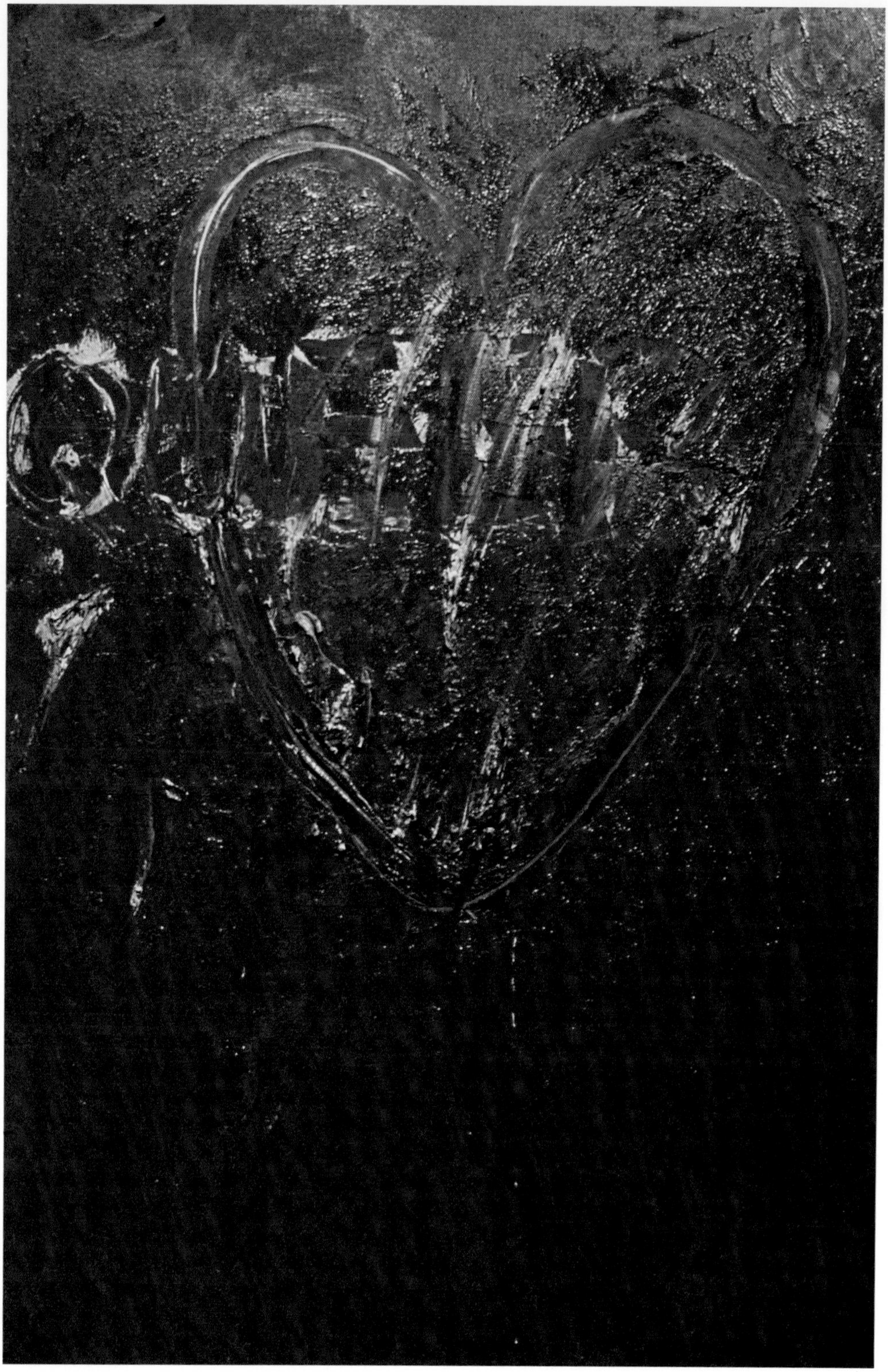

Queer, 1992

Oh Zone, 1992

Acid Rain, 1992

Love Sex Death, 1992 (triptych)

SEX

DEATH

Landscape, 1991

Landscape, 1991

Fuck Me Blind, 1993

Toxo, 1992

Sick, 1992

Kiss, 1992

KY, 1992

Blackmail, 1992

True Blue, 1992

Poofs, 1992

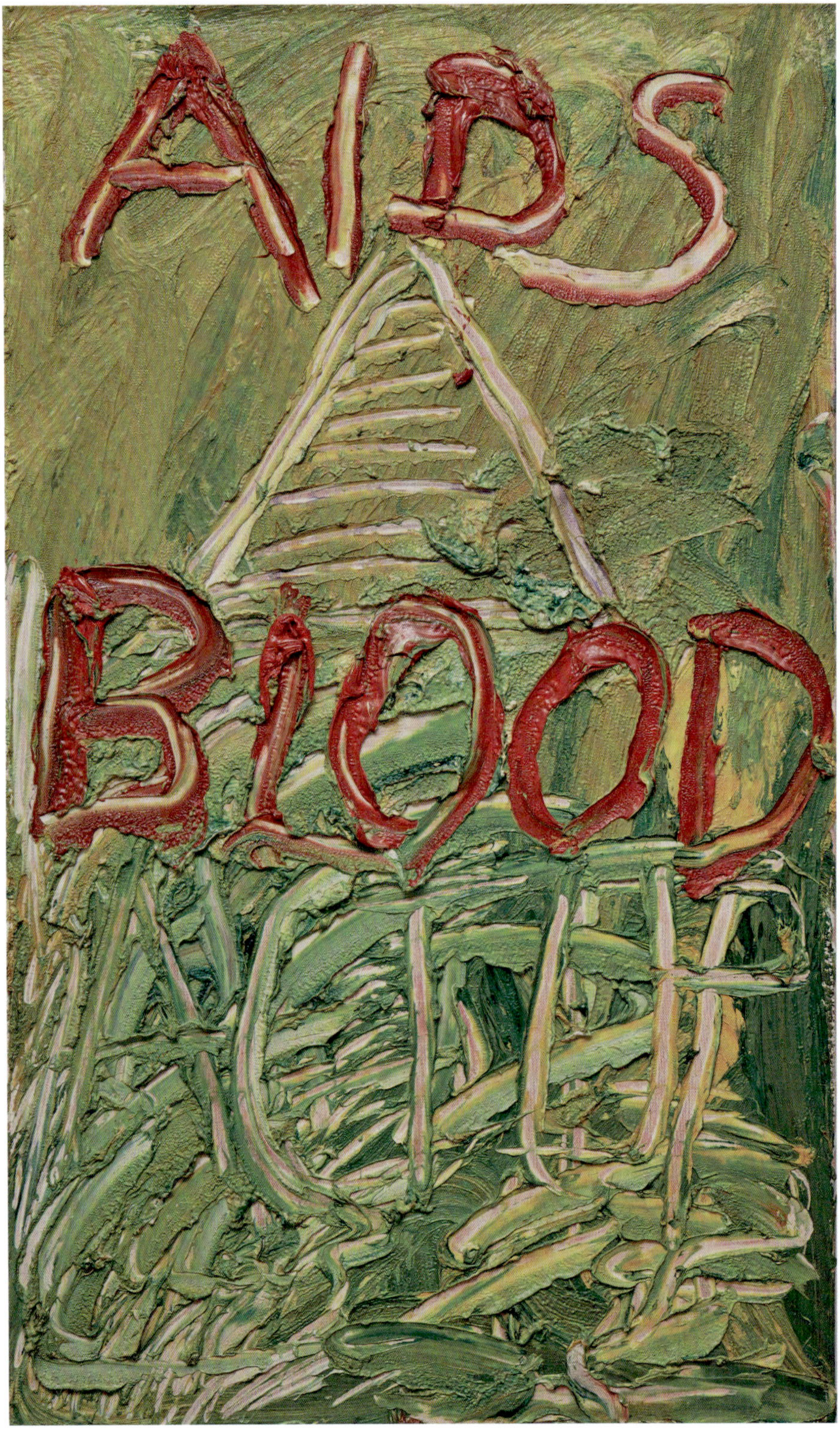

AIDS Blood, 1992

Positive, 1992

EDEN AND GETHSEMANE THE GARDEN AT PROSPECT COTTAGE

MARCO MARTELLA

Derek Jarman, Prospect Cottage, 1992

In his last text, written in the twilight of his life, Derek Jarman noted: 'Paradise haunts all gardens, and some gardens are paradises.'[1] His, he knew, was one of those. One could almost doubt that it was a real garden, unfenced as it is, blending imperceptibly into the surrounding arid landscape, open to the winds and storms of the nearby sea. It is a singular garden indeed: overflowing, full of colour, born of a vision of beauty pursued to the end. If death is present, it is because the garden seems to welcome life in its entirety, brazenly, as only a work of art can do. Or gardening, when it becomes art.

Jarman bought Prospect Cottage in 1987, a place he discovered on a visit to the Dungeness area of Kent with his companion Keith Collins and the actress Tilda Swinton in 1986. It was just one of the many fishermen's cottages that dot the desolate plain of Dungeness, at the foot of a large nuclear power station. 1986 was a turning point in his life. He had just learned that he was HIV-positive, at a time when AIDS was still poorly understood and there was no treatment to combat it. He did not have much time left; everything had to be reassessed, including his work as an artist. A new phase in his life was beginning, and little did he know that a garden was waiting for him.

During the eight years he had left to live – this 'borrowed time', as he called it, this 'reprieve' that life granted him – Prospect Cottage became the pivotal point of his existence. The more virulent his illness became, the more, it would seem, his artistic activity intensified: films, painting, writing, set design, video clips. A bit like trees that, feeling threatened by a deadly parasite or drought, start to flower abundantly, even out of season. It was in gardening, as he himself said, that this creative vitality found its ideal humus. In 1989, when asked by a journalist about the continuity between his different artistic activities, he replied: 'It's all very intuitive; gardening is at the centre [...] It's what I should always have done. I shouldn't have become involved in cinema. That's for fools! Gardening is central because with gardening, one is entering another time... eternal returns and cycles. Those are the resurrectional cycles in my life; planting a seed and watching it come up.'[2]

The garden was a recurring theme in the work of these years. It is present in *The Garden* (1990), his film about AIDS, where it forms part of the naive, enchanted world in

1 Derek Jarman, *Derek Jarman's Garden*, Thames & Hudson, London 1995, p. 40.
2 Mark Kidel, 'A Conversation with Derek Jarman' [1989], in *Pleased to Meet You*, no. 11, September 2021, Semiose éditions, p. 6.

which the two young protagonists experience happiness, and which the disease, like the serpent of Paradise, will destroy. It appears several times in his book dedicated to colours, *Chroma: A Book of Colour – June '93* (1994); it is the backdrop to his journals, published under the titles *Modern Nature* (1991) and *Smiling in Slow Motion* (2000), and the subject of his last text, *Derek Jarman's Garden* (1995). As for the paintings of the final years, red is as much a reference to blood and disease as to the poppies in the garden. His *Black Paintings* (1986–1991), too, filled with (dried) flowers and disparate objects from the beach at Dungeness – pebbles, bits of branches, scrap metal – evoke Prospect Cottage. But the garden is much more than a recurring presence, a link between the works, or one more work in the protean landscape of Jarman's late production. It is the vital core, radiating the energy needed to nourish creation and life itself. The very centre.

When Jarman bought Prospect Cottage, the idea of a garden was still remote, if not unthinkable. The climate in Dungeness is particularly difficult: dry and very hot in summer, windy and icy in winter. Only a few weeds survive in the shingle soil. What is more, a garden needs time to grow, and Jarman was out of time. Nonetheless, he began to design mineral beds in front of the house, first by placing pieces of brick found in the ground and then pebbles picked up on the beach: circles and squares forming an initial garden, a formal garden 'à la française', he said, but inert. Behind the house, he planted a dog rose, probably found nearby, using a piece of driftwood as a stake. With this gesture, the garden began.

He found his childhood gardening tools, which he had never thrown away, in a trunk. He relearned how to garden by rediscovering the names of the plants, their habits and their requirements. He also rediscovered the memories of the beautiful gardens he knew, starting with Villa Zuassa, on Lake Maggiore, Italy, where he had lived as a child with his parents, where he had played naked with his sister and had fallen in love

Outline for the planting of Jarman's garden in Dungeness, from the notebook *Garden Book I*, 1989

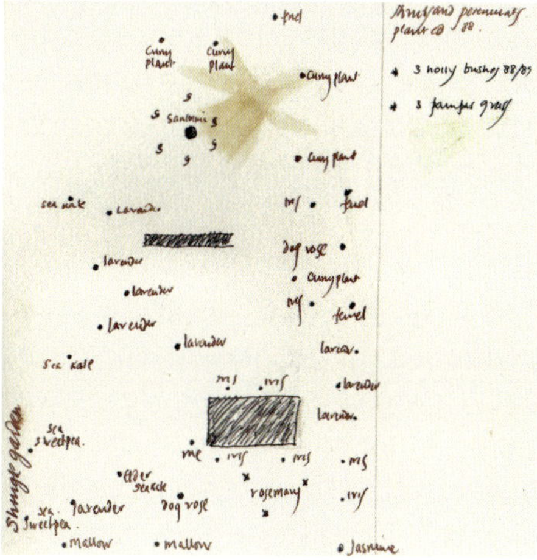

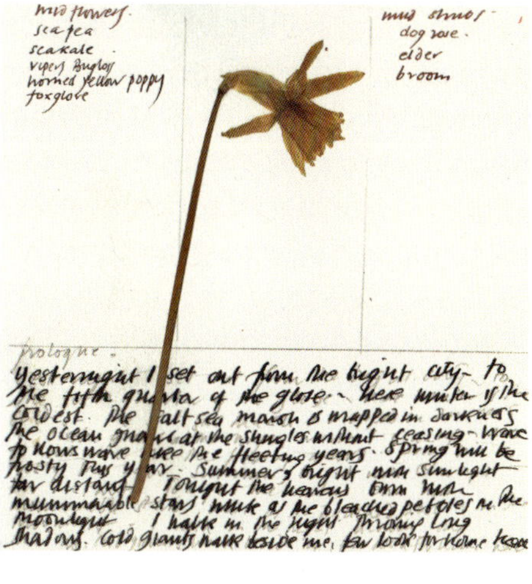

with Davide, the housekeeper's son, who took him on bike rides through the countryside. And his family's garden, where his father taught him how to sow seeds. And he set about planting the garden at Prospect Cottage. In holes dug in the shingle, filled with good soil and manure bought from a nearby farm, he dug in plants found wild in the surrounding area or from the excellent nurseries in Kent. Before long, to the surprise of the gardener himself, the garden was bursting with flowers.

Jarman was an instinctive gardener, an artist who pursued his vision to the end, but he was also a judicious, even excellent gardener. You only have to take a quick glance at the vegetal palette at Prospect Cottage to see this. The plants are carefully chosen, adapted to the climate and the poor soil: lavender, santolina, broom, valerian, borage, elder, marigold, immortelle, orpine... One day, while he was gardening, some visitors arrived at Prospect Cottage who seemed particularly interested in his plantations. They were Christopher Lloyd and Beth Chatto, two famous English gardeners who were out walking in Dungeness.[3] At first intimidated, Jarman answered their questions about his flowers, and then they discussed gardening. Lloyd wrote about Jarman's garden on several occasions, and Chatto drew inspiration from it when she planted her dry garden at home.

The colours of the flowers are bright, even garish. Jarman did not like the delicate pastel tones of gardening magazines. He preferred the bright reds, electric blues, oranges and yellows of the burnt landscapes of the south. It is because this garden wants to be *seen*.[4] Here we find his taste for strong contrasts, but also an echo of the political commitment of those years and the fight against the silence that British society cast over AIDS and those who were dying of it.

Alongside the flowers, the garden is filled with necklaces of pebbles and shells, driftwood planted in the ground, scrap metal and barbed wire, debris picked up on the beach and collected like treasures. The magic that Jarman often tries to evoke in his films emerges spontaneously in the garden of Prospect Cottage thanks to the artist's simple, playful gesture: 'It isn't a gloomy garden, its circles and squares have a sense of humour – a fairy ring for troglodytic pixies – the stones a notation for a long-forgotten music, an ancestral sound to which I add a few new notes each morning.'[5]

3 Christopher Lloyd (1921–2006); Beth Chatto (1923–2018).

4 When I drove to Dungeness, I remember spotting Prospect Cottage from a distance, such was the contrast between this brightly coloured spot and the surrounding arid landscape.

5 Derek Jarman, *Modern Nature* [1991], The Overlook Press, Woodstock, New York 1994, p. 177.

The result is a garden brimming with plants, rocky, wild and strangely open to the desolate landscape that Jarman loved, as if he wanted to welcome the Dungeness plain into its bosom. 'My garden's boundaries', he wrote, 'are the horizon.'[6]

Prospect Cottage was above all 'a therapy and a pharmacopoeia',[7] the place where healing is possible.

In a poem, Jarman wrote: 'I built my garden with the colours of healing'.[8] He was fascinated by medicinal plants and the magical beliefs that were once associated with them. If sage (*salvia*) is marvellous in his eyes, it is not just because of its mauve flowers nor its resistance to drought, but because it is the plant that *saves*. During his long stays in London hospitals, he recounted in his journals that he thought about his garden, which might simultaneously be facing a storm or drought. Sometimes he thought about the planting or sowing he would do the following spring if the illness allowed. Every gardener knows: a garden, even the simplest one, is an act of faith. By projecting us into the future, it nourishes hope. And it takes care of the gardener who takes care of it.

Little by little, Prospect Cottage became a place of resistance in the face of illness and despondency. The cycle of death and rebirth of the annual flowers or the *Crambe maritima* – a plant that grows wild in Dungeness, withers in winter and is reborn in spring to fill the plain with its heady scent – seems to belie the inevitability of death, its finality. The pleasure of feeling the earth between his fingers, of seeing a seed germinate, the gardener's wonder at his plants standing valiantly against the wind, tending to beauty, however ephemeral and fragile it may be – all this makes the garden an enclosure not of survival, but of life, and of life in superabundance. So much so that, at times, Prospect Cottage finally became the promised Eden. 'My paradise at the fifth quarter', as he called it. Or, 'our corner of Paradise, the part of the garden the Lord forgot to mention'.[9]

This is not an evocation, and even less a metaphor, of Eden, but a true Eden: the desirable place, the place where life is good, the place of delights still unaware of death.

However, the garden never cured anything. In the moments when the disease worsened or death drew ever closer day by day, it could do almost nothing. When the postman

6 Ibid., p. 3.
7 Derek Jarman, *Derek Jarman's Garden*, p. 12.
8 Derek Jarman, *Chroma: A Book of Colour – June '93*, Century, London 1994.
9 Derek Jarman, *Modern Nature*, p. 23.

brought Jarman letters announcing the death of one of his HIV-positive friends in a London or New York hospital, Prospect Cottage darkened: 'I water the roses and wonder whether I will see them bloom. I plant my herbal garden as a panacea, read up on all the aches and pains that plants will cure – and know they are not going to help. The garden as pharmacopoeia has failed.'[10]

The scrap metal and driftwood he continued to pick up on the beach became crosses, rough headstones that turned the garden into a cemetery, albeit a flowery one, brimming with life. The pebble beds became 'lovers' knots',[11] in memory of departed friends, so that the more death was present, the more the garden filled with plants, sculptures in wood, rubber or rusty iron, and ghosts.

> I walk in this garden
> holding the hands of dead friends.
> Old age came quickly for my frosted generation,
> cold, cold, cold, they died so silently.[12]

The place of delights is transformed into a place of pain:

> Here at the sea's edge
> I have planted my dragon-toothed garden
> to defend the porch,
> steadfast warriors
> against those who protest their impropriety
> even to the end of the world.
> A fathomless lethargy has swallowed me,
> great waves of doubt broken me,
> all my thoughts washed away.
> The storms have blown salt tears,
> burning my garden,
> Gethsemane and Eden.[13]

Gethsemane is the Garden of Olives in Jerusalem, where Christ spent his night of agony before being arrested. However, when it becomes Gethsemane, the garden is perhaps even closer to the gardener. A complicity, at times a true brotherhood, is established between the gardener and his plants, which are also subject to the eternal struggle of all living beings against

10 Ibid., p. 179.
11 Ibid., p. 55.
12 Derek Jarman, *Derek Jarman's Garden*, p. 81
13 Ibid., p. 82.

death. Like when, one morning in January, he came across a small borage plant in his garden that had blossomed well before its time: the flower, in the process of wilting in the morning frost, but immediately afterwards, no doubt thanks to a ray of sunshine, reared its head again. Jarman wrote in his journal: 'I, borage, bring courage.'[14]

Eden and Gethsemane. It is impossible to imagine one without the other.

In this way, as gardener and artist, Jarman explored the mystery of mysteries, the mystery of time, life and death, the mystery of resurrection. By planting and watering his garden, he learned that death is inscribed in the very time of nature: the eternally repeated time of the seasons, the time of the growth of a blade of grass or a shrub, the time of dead leaves that turn into humus destined to nourish other plants, or the time of annual flowers, living for only one summer to produce seeds that the wind will carry elsewhere. Seen in this wider context, death appears in a new light, and sometimes becomes acceptable.

But there is an even more dizzying time, an otherworldly time that appears as if by magic in the garden:

> The gardener digs in another time, without past or future, beginning or end. A time that does not cleave the day with rush hours, lunch breaks, the last bus home. As you walk in the garden you pass into this time – the moment of entering can never be remembered. Around you the landscape lies transfigured. Here is the Amen beyond the prayer [...] I'm brought suddenly back to the here and now by the shrill argumentative voice of the phone. My Person from Perlock is on the line, talking of time with beginning and end, literal time, monotheist time, for which you are unfailingly charged.[15]

In one of his last poems, Jarman asked his garden: 'Will you be coming next year?'

14 Derek Jarman, *Modern Nature*, p. 4. This is an English saying based on the Latin *Ego borago gaudia semper ago*, a phrase shouted by Roman soldiers as they prepared for battle by drinking borage wine.

15 Ibid., p. 30.

The garden at Prospect Cottage has never stopped flowering. The winds of Dungeness sweep through it in winter and its flowers stand up valiantly to the drought of summer. The site is perfectly preserved and the plants that Jarman planted are still alive, even if the garden has been turned into a memorial since its gardener is no longer there, and his companion Keith Collins, who looked after it after his death, has also passed away. This is the fate of every artist's garden. How do you keep a work of art alive? What gives Prospect Cottage its poetic depth is the gesture with which Jarman planted and tended it. A gesture cannot be preserved. It can only be evoked in images, in words, in memory. Despite this, it is wonderful that, with the support of friends such as Tilda Swinton, a Trust was set up to buy Prospect Cottage and prevent the garden from disappearing. The site has become an artists' residence, and an excellent gardener is in charge of looking after the plants.

This garden will therefore continue to question us about the way we look at plants, the earth and the landscape today. What does nature mean to us in an age of pandemics, wars and predicted ecological disasters? How can 'modern nature' give us courage, provide us with something to oppose fear, discouragement and death?

Perhaps the answer is simple. It is hidden in the gesture with which, despite the headwinds, a gardener puts a seed in the ground, takes care of the sprouting plant and watches it grow.

The Garden, 1990

CRUISING THE HETEROTOPIA ON HAMPSTEAD HEATH

Sex on the Heath is an idyll pre-fall.
—Derek Jarman

CY LECERF MAULPOIX

On 22 March 1989, Derek Jarman walked up a steep cliffside path in the village of Hordle in Hampshire, the area where he spent his childhood. A few dozen deep purple violets nestled in a small recess. Flowers of secrecy, associated in his journal *Modern Nature* (1991) with the cult of Demeter and adolescent men, they bring back memories of an encounter with another classmate, in a garden hidden from view, during his years at boarding school. The first physical feelings of the two young boys, naked in the spring sun, where violets and skin intertwine, are experienced as an inaugural experience, a sensory symphony between the human and non-human worlds. 'A new orchard and garden was mine',[1] he wrote at the time. For him, the flowering garden became a symbol of pure enjoyment, of an authentic relationship with the world and with others, before external shame and social condemnation set in: that of his grandmother, who accused violets of corrupting the air and heralding death, or the homophobic violence inflicted by other boarding-school classmates when they discovered his relationship with his friend.

If there were primordial experiences for Jarman, the suspended time-space of a living, enclosed garden, at the very heart of a reality that held homosexual eroticism and its symbols as perverse or moribund, inaugurated a heterotopia where desire and landscape intermingled.[2] Jarman would never cease to cherish and pursue it as an adult.

Many years after this seminal episode, the artist, gardener and film-maker had become a compulsive walker. He wandered London and its outskirts, following the paths of desirous cartographies like many other generations of men before him. He wandered into parks at dusk to enjoy the landscape and its furtive inhabitants.

Even if 'location is the key to respectability',[3] Jarman, who was never in search of respectability, rejected the intimacy of the commercial spaces that were springing up all over the English capital. While he was no stranger to the feverish bars of Soho and the city's more subdued clubs and saunas, they lacked the flavour and power of shady alleys and bush-bedecked

1 Derek Jarman, *Modern Nature: The Journals of Derek Jarman* [1991], The Overlook Press, Woodstock, New York 1994, p. 38.
2 Theorised by Michel Foucault in 1967, the concept of heterotopia refers to a space characterised by its discontinuity with its surroundings. A closed or enclosed space, heterotopia can also refer to the physical location of utopia or, in any case, of places emancipated from the usual norms that allow new freedoms or new rules to emerge.
3 Jarman, *Modern Nature*, p. 83.

Prospect Cottage, 2018

detours. Despite the history of the social hygiene movement and social control they embody, parks, especially Hampstead Heath, are landscapes marked by many dissident uses, resistant to sexual morality. Sex workers, drug addicts and men in search of other men rub shoulders on the margins and edges. Located to the north of the city, Hampstead Heath is wilder than other London parks, and is not enclosed. The darkness of the forest paths and discreet clearings disturb the surface of an old homophile pastoral dream.[4] Ambushes, homophobic murders, blackmail and police assaults irrevocably haunt the Heath, 'a symbol of the dark into which the gay world has been driven by heterosexual censure'.[5]

Yet, in Hampstead Heath, he adds, 'the alfresco fuck is the original fuck. Didn't the Garden of Eden come before the house which hid our nakedness? Sex on the Heath is an idyll pre-fall.' Jarman fucks on the Heath after dark and appropriates the political utopia of his predecessors. In the deviant landscapes of homosexual desire, he glimpses the possibility of an alternative community. A chaotic, Dionysian, impertinent community, a world away from the respectable homosexuality that he rejects. 'In the dark for a brief moment, age, class, wealth, all the barriers are down. An illusion you say, I know, but what a sweet one.'[6]

Jarman knew that the epidemic was snaking everywhere. Years went by. Even when he contracted the virus, he continued to visit the Heath tirelessly. In his last notebooks, which make up the text of *Smiling in Slow Motion*, written between 1991 and 1994, he recounts the day-to-day loss of friends and lovers simultaneously, and more profoundly, inscribes death in the landscapes of everyday life. When illness 'gives a finality to every gesture', returning to Hampstead Heath was sometimes like walking through the ruins of a golden age. 'Is this the last flower I will plant?' he wondered. 'Will this be my last flying trip into my past – the Heath. I go to spite the present.'[7]

On a July evening in 1991, Jarman wrote: 'I spent most of the night on the Heath talking to a charming silver-haired man about the past and the razoring that the city has performed here, all the undergrowth burned. The Heath used to belong to the GLC[8] and was unkempt and romantic; now under the force of finance, it has received a banker's barbering.'[9] Although it

4 In the 19th and early 20th centuries, inspired in particular by the ancient pastoral myths of Theocritus and Virgil's *Bucolics*, theorists, poets and artists such as Walt Whitman, Edward Carpenter and John Addington Symonds turned to so-called 'natural' landscapes – parks, ponds, forests and rivers – as places where a democratic, trans-class community of comrades could emerge. This return of homosexuality to the real or fantasised landscapes of nature revealed a desire as much as a strategic approach – that of exorcising the shame and stigma of sexualities considered unnatural, of 're-naturalising' the homosexual experience while at the same time proposing a political utopia. See Matt Cook, '"A New City of Friends": London and Homosexuality in the 1890s', in *London and the Culture of Homosexuality, 1885–1914*, Cambridge University Press, Cambridge 2003.

5 Here and following quote: Derek Jarman, *Modern Nature*, p. 83.

6 Ibid., p. 84.

7 Here and previous quote: Derek Jarman, *Smiling in Slow Motion: Journals, 1991–1994* [2000], Vintage, London 2001, p. 33–34.

8 The GLC was the Greater London Council, the main local government administrative body for Greater London from 1965 to 1986.

9 Here and following quote: Derek Jarman, *Smiling in Slow Motion*, p. 30.

is not a question of nuclear radiation, as at Prospect Cottage, the aesthetics of control and domestication of life under a capitalist regime links the artist's body and the landscape to a process of irremediable destruction.

Yet, as with Prospect Cottage, the experience of the Heath resists this melancholy. Jarman is reunited with friends, strangers and fans who populate an eternal stage of theatre and cinema.[10] The erotic and mischievous force of the nocturnal communities that move about on Hampstead Heath encouraged the multiplication of scenes that were sometimes sensual and sometimes comic. Jarman continued to enjoy, as an artist, actor and/or spectator, what unfolded before him. 'The leather boys clustered around a rather handsome lad who had stripped off: pale and finely built, he was showered with kisses. Lightening played through the night, a voice in the half-light said: "It's electric here."' he wrote on this same hot July night.

In February 1993, BBC journalist Jeremy Isaacs asked Jarman about the risks of anonymous sex on Hampstead Heath in a filmed interview. Always a fighter against the siren song of the self-righteous of the time, Jarman maintained the idea of community to talk about the collective experience on the Heath. In his diaries, however, he confided his difficulties: 'I find myself hesitating on the questions of sex on the Heath. How anonymous is anonymous? A hornet's nest of taboo sex, HIV, casual partners, this is one you can't win.'[11] In an era characterised by stigmatisation and the urgent need for community self-organisation in the face of indifferent public authorities and their rejection, could Jarman really appreciate the complicity he shared with this world?

In the short graduation film *The Clearing* (1993) by the young Greek director Alexis Bistikas,[12] made four months later on Hampstead Heath, Jarman suddenly appears around a bend in the path. The page recounting the day's filming indicates new losses, and the observation that 'the whole world [is] staggering into the grave just a little too soon'.[13] Like Bistikas, Jarman was

Film stills from *The Clearing* (1993) by Alexis Bistikas

10 In June 1989, he encountered the film shoot of an adaptation of Shakespeare's *A Midsummer's Night Dream* (1605).
11 Ibid., p. 306.
12 Alexis Bistikas (1964–1995). His film *The Clearing* (1993) can be seen at www.youtube.com/watch?v=20hTjCIgs4w (last accessed September 2024). Keith Collins also appears in the film.
13 Derek Jarman, *Smiling in Slow Motion*, p. 359.

particularly ill that day. His tired face shows signs of the disease, his emotions suspended in the requiem of a saxophone held by his companion Keith Collins. His loving gaze nevertheless pierces the twilight that hangs over this short film in black and white. It is a reminder, if one were needed, that the Heath is a place of love.

'I chained myself to this landscape', Jarman wrote about Prospect Cottage in *Modern Nature*.[14] In the same way, he is irremediably attached to the fringes of Hampstead Heath. At the very heart of the storm, he knew that the landscapes of desire exist and flourish through the darkness. But he also knew that they were the very condition of his emancipation, of the return of that vital impulse where erotic power and the power of death are experienced, intertwined and confronted.

14 Derek Jarman, *Modern Nature*, p. 77.

Derek Jarman, Prospect Cottage, 1992

PROSPECT COTTAGE

DUNGENESS, KENT, SINCE 1986

The photographs reproduced on pages 135–147 were taken by Richard Deacon, Luke Fowler, Claire Le Restif, Geraint Lewis, Benoît Piéron and Howard Sooley between 1992 and 2023.

Prospect Cottage, 1992

Prospect Cottage and Dungeness, 2021

Derek Jarman, Prospect Cottage, 1992

Prospect Cottage, 2019

CHARLES NAPIER
10 MARZO

Berwick St. Films
The Tempest.
dir. Derek Jarman. cam. Peter Middleton
SLATE
TAKE
ROLL
38

Prospect Cottage, 2023

Prospect Cottage, 2023

Prospect Cottage, 1992

RELIEFS 1987–1991

Nightlife, 1987

Untitled, 1989

A PLANT, 1988

Dead Souls Whisper, 1987

Untitled, 1987

Untitled (Bone, Face and Cross), 1988

Untitled, 1988

Archaeology, 1988

Untitled (Gold Bible), 1990

At the Fifth Quarter of the Globe, 1988

Jumble Sale, 1990

Untitled (Comb), 1989

Untitled (Technico), 1989

CMV Virus (Sight Oh Megalo), 1992

Prospect (Et in Arcadia Ego), 1992

Death is All Things We See Awake, 1991

The Bridge of Sighs, 1987

Every Thought, 1987

Untitled (Red Crucified Figure), 1991

The Common Prayer, 1989

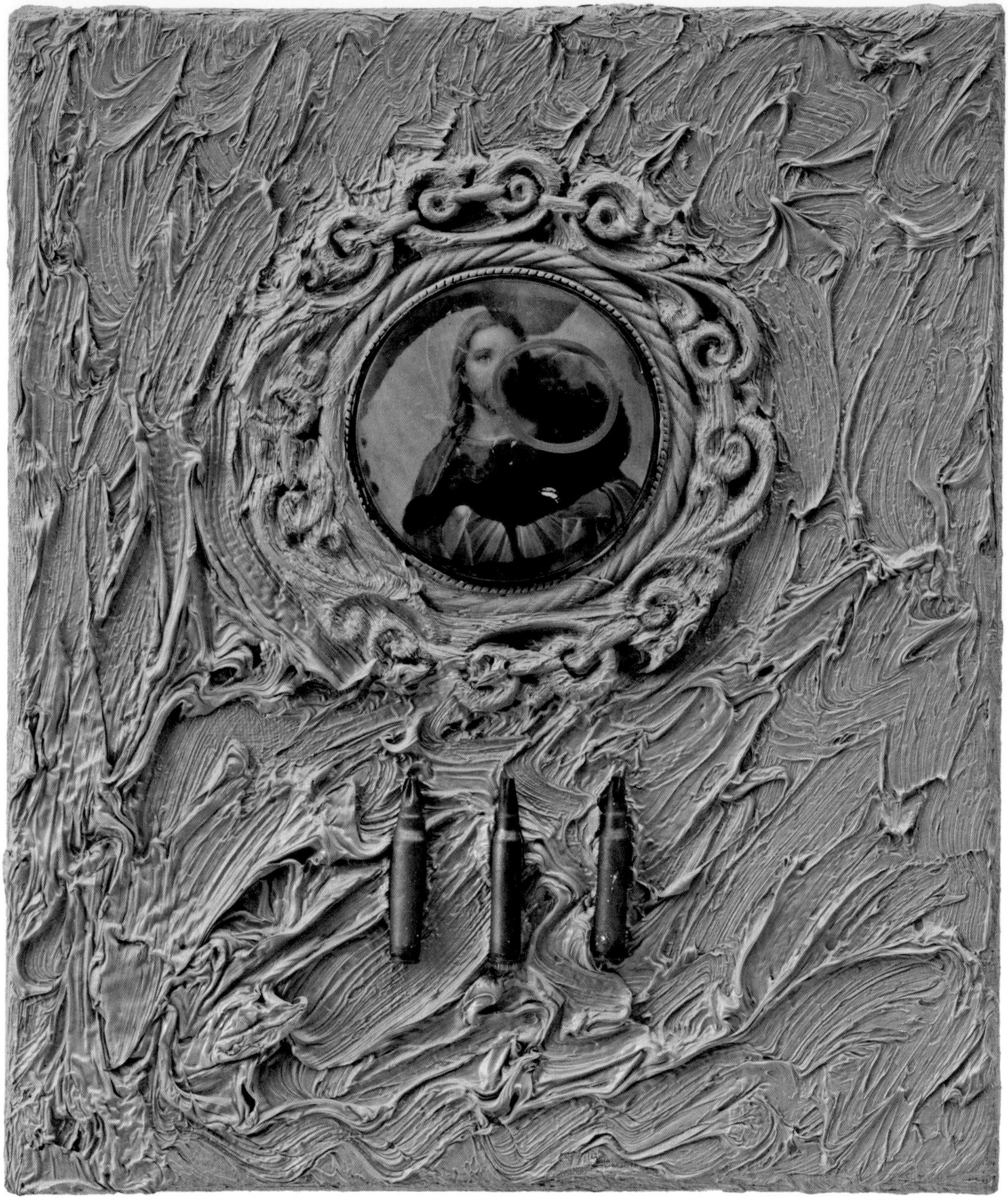

Flesh Tint, 1990

Household God VI (Nelson), 1989

Household God V (Molière), 1989

Household God III (Wagner), 1989

Household God I (Handel), 1989

Household God II (Mozart), 1989

On the set of *The Garden*, 1990

A SOCIAL WAY OF MAKING FILMS

A CONVERSATION WITH JAMES MACKAY AND LAETITIA CHAUVIN

James Mackay during the production of the opera *L'ispirazione* directed by Derek Jarman, Florence, 1988

THE BEGINNINGS OF THE COLLABORATION; VIDEO ART IN THE 1980S; JARMAN'S BACKGROUND; SUPER-8 VS. 16MM; THE MAKING-OF OF *THE ANGELIC CONVERSATION* (1985)

Laetitia Chauvin How would you define your role with Derek Jarman?

James Mackay It evolved over time. At the beginning I was rolling joints, and I progressed to producing films. [Laughs] No, really, at the beginning it was a common interest in artists' film, particularly in Super-8, which, in the late 1970s, was the film medium that most of the younger artists were using. And many of the older artists too! Because of the cost of 16mm films, a lot of the experimental stuff was being filmed and edited on Super-8. I attended a fine art course at North East London Polytechnic, which was more focused on film and video as opposed to other things. After that I hitched a lift to Berlin at the time of the film festival and met Manfred Salzgeber and Alf Bold, who were running different parts of the festival and who would come to be great supporters of the work that I was to do with Derek. It was an amazing experience; I saw lots of exciting new works. Fellini gave me a ticket for *Casanova*, which I had to skip as there was a screening of new Super-8 at the same time. After that I went back to London and became involved with the running of the London Film-Makers' Co-op cinema.[1] I started to program films there as well as other events, including one of the first performances by Throbbing Gristle. By that time I was programming work for Lynda Myles at the Edinburgh Film Festival and the Gregors in Berlin. It was a great time as it was a very open period, and was very friendly and welcoming. It was really an education to be involved in all of that.

LC You were very young then, and yet already had many responsibilities?

JM I was 23 when I was running and programming the Film Co-op cinema. I was really foolhardy, doubling the screenings, but then I had the energy of youth! At that time there was an exhibition in Berlin called *Film as Film*,[2] which was devised by Wilhelm and Birgit Hein, both very important experimental film-makers. The exhibition was brought to

* James Mackay is an independent film producer and curator who worked with Derek Jarman extensively from the 1980s until his death, and produced many of his films, including *The Angelic Conversation* (1985), *The Last of England* (1987) and *Blue* (1993).

** All the names mentioned in this conversation are the subject of a short biographical note at the end of this volume.

1 The London Film-Makers' Co-op, or LFMC, was a British film-making workshop founded in 1966 by, among others, Stephen Dwoskin and Bob Cobbing, and was inspired by Jonas Mekas' Film-Makers' Cooperative in New York. The LFMC was organised as an egalitarian, worksharing co-operative, which assisted production as well as distribution. Work produced by members of the LFMC in the late 1960s and early 1970s has been labelled structural/materialist film. The LFMC ceased to exist in 1999 when it merged with London Video Arts to form LUX.

2 The *Film as Film* exhibition was held in Cologne, Berlin, Essen and Stuttgart in 1977, and in London in 1979.

London, in a modified form, by David Curtis and Simon Field, and the screenings were spread between the Film Co-op, the Hayward Gallery and the National Film Theatre. It was backed by the Arts Council and the government, so the event brought together a wide range of experimental film-makers from across the globe. We had people like Stan Brackhage, Danièle Huillet and Jean-Marie Straub, Carolee Schneemann, Kurt Kren and Takahiko Iimura, everybody you could think of at that time. I was given the task of looking after Paul Sharits, which was a revelation. He was a really wonderful man, but he was difficult. It was very hard to get him out of the pub to attend things in time. But I learned a lot listening to him. I think he is one of the greatest film-makers of the 20th century, really. It was a brilliant time because there were all those people around. However, at the time and for a long time afterwards, experimental film wasn't considered fine art. It was considered an 'art' like cinema is an art, but it wasn't considered part of the fine art canon. It wasn't considered to be on the same level as opera, and certainly not as painting or sculpture. But the work that was coming out of, let's say England, was stunning. There was Malcolm Le Grice, Peter Gidal, Guy Sherwin, Lis Rhodes, lots and lots of really interesting artists who had been working in film since the mid-1960s. That was in the late 1970s. It wasn't until the 1990s that the moving image finally became accepted as an art. By that time its history had been ignored. You get some new artists now who might make a film that is very like a film made in the 1960s without knowing it. There was a lot of reinventing the wheel going on, because I suppose the galleries didn't have access to the original work and the past artists. I come from a period when the moving image was considered to be like a subsection of commercial cinema.

LC How did you meet Jarman in 1978?

JM Derek was part of the conversation. Peter Wollen, Gidal, Rhodes, all these people were writing and debating, and Derek was involved in a certain area of that. He wasn't part of the structuralist movement, which was the dominant movement at the time. He wasn't really part of the other avant-garde movement, the one that came from the French Nouvelle Vague, represented in the UK by Wollen and Laura Mulvey.

Derek was his own movement, a bit like Jeff Keen in Brighton. Derek was very amiable and very interested in other film-makers. He had a long correspondence with Kenneth Anger, but he also knew John Du Cane, an interesting and important film-maker from the 1970s – who became a disciple of the Maharishi and took the name 'Rishi' – as well as others. Derek wasn't a trained film director. He didn't have a clue really about cinema conventions, nor did he really care. He came from painting and he was a painter and a set designer until after his work with Ken Russell on *The Devils* (1971). That was his first brush with cinema – still as a designer, not as a film-maker. I think he found the experience quite frightening, the industrial scale of it, which was even bigger than the industrial scale of opera or what he'd done in theatre. I remember when he was designing Russell's production of Stravinsky's *The Rake's Progress*, at the Teatro Della Pergola in Florence in 1982. I was speaking to him on the phone and I asked him, what's it like? And he said: 'Well, they're making 500 pairs of shoes!' Huge productions involved tons of work. He started at the Slade art school in the painting department, but moved to the design department because he found the people more interesting. At that time, all art was very macho; even the Film Co-op had quite a macho atmosphere. It was just starting to change when I got there in the mid-1970s. But I could see there were a lot of beards, a lot of that kind of thing. 16mm was a manly pursuit. Super-8 was a bit...

LC Queer?

JM No, not queer, I don't think there was that kind of prejudice. The first gay film festival in the UK organised by Bruno de Florence was held at the Film Co-op, but that work wasn't considered serious. If you were a 'serious' film-maker at the Film Co-op, you would be making structuralist films in 16mm. Derek was a painter and he had exhibited at the Lisson Gallery which was founded in 1967 by Nicholas Logsdail, who had been a fellow student at the Slade. Derek encouraged him when he wanted to open a gallery and helped him

On the set of *The Garden*, 1990

get the space and helped him with hammer and nails to get it to work. As a consequence, Derek had one of the early exhibitions at Lisson. But then, when he moved into cinema, however strange and esoteric Derek's films like *Sebastiane* (1976) and *Jubilee* (1978) were, I think they felt he was turning his back on painting. People stopped seeing him as a fine artist. That's when I met him, at the end of the 1970s just as he finished making *The Tempest* (1979), when he wasn't part of the fine art world, but he was still making these amazing films on the margins of cinema. There was a clear division between what he said were commissioned works like *The Tempest* or *Caravaggio* (1986) and his personal cinema of Super-8.

LC What was your involvement in Jarman's projects?

JM It's hard to define because initially it was just a question of trying to find a way to conserve the Super-8 films, which are very fragile, and trying to get them exhibited. We tried lots of different things. The Berlin Film Festival Forum paid for a blowup from Super-8 to 16mm of *In the Shadow of the Sun* (1972–1974), in 1981, for instance. One of the very first things I did with Derek was at the Barbican in London. A friend of Derek's, Brian Montgomery, who, with his brother, was involved in book fairs, put on the first art fair in London there. It must have been in 1981 or 1982. They gave Derek a stall there. Derek sent me to this art exhibition with a monitor and a videotape player, to show *In the Shadow of the Sun*. That's all I had. I was there for two days, just standing there, and there was no interest at all, apart from this one man who came up to me at one point and started asking all these questions: 'What do you hope to achieve by screening this film here?' etc. I didn't know what to answer, because there were no collectors. You gave your film to the Film Co-op or to Canyon Cinema, for instance, and they showed it in colleges and elsewhere. Even public gallery screenings were rare. I had an interesting conversation with this visitor and later when Derek

In the Shadow of the Sun, 1972–1974

enquired about the fair, I described this one visitor. He said, 'Oh, yes, Jacob Rothschild, an old friend of mine.' Indeed, Jacob Rothschild was a great collector of contemporary art.

LC Was it the first thing you did together?

JM No, we did other little things. We took *In the Shadow of the Sun* to Berlin, and then to other festivals. I was trying to get Derek's films transferred to 16mm and had success with three of the shorter ones. It was quite hard to raise money even though the amounts of money we were looking for were laughably small, tiny even, but it was still quite a lot of money to us as we didn't have any. After a while we thought: 'Well, why are we doing this and not making new films?' Derek had got stuck with his aborted sci-fi film project *Neutron* (c. 1983) and *Caravaggio*. One day we were making a videotape of some of the Super-8s for the ICA. They'd given us a space to do this. It was quite a nice, square little room. We were working with one of the technicians, Steve Radmall, filming the Super-8 off the wall onto video. There was an old mirror lying around and Derek said: 'Let's try filming into the mirror.' He set it up and arranged it all. Steve held the mirror. Suddenly, it was really much more fun. A friend of mine who had just left the Royal College of Art, Marek Budzynski, a really good editor, had access to a video editing suite. Marek edited a short piece with Derek – three or four minutes – and we used that to try to interest people to make a longer film.

LC Like a teaser.

JM It was a teaser. We spent the summer of 1984, one or two days every week or two, filming with Philip Williamson and Paul Reynolds, who weren't actors, in different parts of the country. We went down to Dorset and other places. It was a love story by proxy. That became the film *The Angelic Conversation* (1985). The bit that we filmed with Steve Radmall is the centre of it: the moon moving across the screen, which then becomes the oculus of the Pantheon in Rome. It is exactly as it was edited by Marek as a teaser. We still couldn't get the money. It was very difficult.

FILM PRODUCTION: FINANCING INDEPENDENT FILMS; FOUNDING BASILISK COMMUNICATIONS; THE JOY ON JARMAN'S FILM SET

LC You were neither an archivist nor a producer per se, but rather a multi-tasker and helper on all possible levels, both administrative and artistic?

JM We were a film community. I worked on other people's films as well. Everyone was very collaborative, working with each other on their projects. I am one of nature's organisers.

LC For *The Angelic Conversation*, you started to play a different role. You were the producer, trying to find money.

JM Yes, but there weren't any complex financial formulas involved. It was just a question of going to funding bodies or patrons and getting some cash. It was quite straightforward. For *The Angelic Conversation*, we were working under the auspices of the production board of the British Film Institute (BFI), which at that time was run by Peter Sainsbury. He helped us out both on *The Angelic Conversation* and *Imagining October* (1984). It wasn't like a business. They were filmed by myself and Derek, especially *The Angelic Conversation*. We both had cameras and the whole film expedition would be a driver, one of the actors – we never had the two together until the last weekend – and myself and Derek. That would be the whole thing. We would go somewhere and we would film. It was a different way of working and it wasn't funded. It wasn't even treated by the BFI as a film, more as a research project.

Imagining October, 1984

LC What was the collaboration with the BFI like?

JM Sainsbury was very supportive, but then he had to leave. Later it became much more difficult to work with the BFI. On the one hand, the BFI was supporting Derek, they wanted to make *Caravaggio*. But at the same time, they wanted to suppress *The Angelic Conversation* because they thought that somehow it would denigrate this commercial film that they were trying to make. That was really stupid... We had to take *The Angelic Conversation* to Berlin ourselves. Fortunately, both Derek and I were really well liked by the festival there and we had a lot of friends supporting us. We showed it at the Berlin Film Festival and then other places. For a film that was made by two idiots and two cameras, it was quite successful internationally! [Laughs] Then Derek made *Caravaggio*.

LC You were not the producer of that film.

JM Well, early on, I was working on it with Derek. It went through so many different combinations and stages. Derek had *Caravaggio* as a project before I met him. I contributed the script and helped them find things like actors – Spencer Leigh for instance – and the film studio (a warehouse on Canary Wharf). That's just stuff that you did anyway because you were part of the team. But the BFI didn't really want people like me, they wanted more commercial people. After the Sainsbury period, I think the BFI started to think: 'How can we make money out of this? How can we take this very strange, eccentric English film-maker and make it in the world of Cannes and Hollywood? How can it work there?' That's really what they were aiming for. I don't think they ever understood Derek's work. They didn't think about his other work as painting or his design work. I didn't fit into that because I did understand Derek's work and I did understand where he came from. He made *Caravaggio*, but he was very unhappy because it was one compromise after another. He wanted to do certain things, they wouldn't let him. That's why afterwards I had to learn how to run a company. We made *The Last of England* (1987), which actually opens with Spring Rupert Audley frottaging on top of the Caravaggio painting *Amor vincit omnia* (Love Conquers All, 1601–1602). That was Derek expressing his anger. Maybe because I was naïve and didn't have experience in setting up production and financing, it was easier for me than it would have been for somebody who was an experienced producer. I still had a lot of friends, and they were very helpful. Dagmar Benke from ZDF, the German TV Channel, said she wanted to make a film like *Imagining October*, as short film for ZDF. I was able to convince her it was a better idea to come in on *The Last of England*, and so it got made in a different way. I didn't realise until afterwards that having five or six sources of finance was unusual. Most people got all their money from one place. I suddenly became a sort of celebrity in the world of film finance without really knowing it. We had money from Germany, from Japan, from England. Nobody had done that before.

LC An international production! That was how your independence was assured.

JM It was. We were very lucky because we were able to make *The Last of England* without any interference. There was no compromise.

LC Is that when you founded Basilisk Communications?

JM Not quite. *The Last of England* was produced by a company called Anglo International Films. Along with Derek's *War Requiem* (1989) and *Twenty-One* (1991) directed by Don Boyd, it's the only film that company produced. Derek thought it might be easier if we just used this connection with Don, but it turned out that wasn't the smart thing to do because it meant that someone else owned *The Last of England*. That's when I set up Basilisk with Chris Harrison, who had worked for Don on his films. That meant we had a completely independent vehicle for making films.

LC Did Basilisk Communications produce only Jarman's films?

JM No, they did other things as well, but not much. We had a lot of work with Derek because we were doing music videos, and then *The Garden* (1990) and *Blue* (1993). It was a production company for Derek's work, primarily. The problem when you're making small films is that you're not making any profit. You're only making money in terms of the budget.

You get a fee – a percentage of the budget goes to the company, which is fine with commercials like those for the Pet Shop Boys, The Smiths, all that stuff, fantastic. You make a profit and it's there. But with films like *The Garden*, you're negotiating with Channel 4 and the other financers, and they're saying: 'Well, can't you put your production fee in as part of the budget?' You're having to make the film, but without it being profitable, even at the level of production. Even running a tiny company, it just doesn't work. Even now that Basilisk has *Blue* and *The Garden* and other projects of Derek's, every year I subsidise it to keep it going. Every so often there's a sale to television or something, and that comes back to me, and I start to fund it again. What was really annoying at the time was that Channel 4 set up a workshop scheme based on our model, but would only let us be part of it if we became a group under the official union scheme, so they never gave it to us! Yet we had John Maybury, Cerith Wyn Evans, Richard Heslop and many others, all working in our group. The other film groups were getting a budget to support their activities and we weren't. It was really sad, really mean. Because we'd made a few music videos, they all thought we were making tons of money. At least we were more glamorous than the others! But we were broke. Derek only had money when his father died. That's how he bought Prospect Cottage.

LC In a filmed interview you gave recently for the BFI, you talked very interestingly about how to finance and support and have confidence in film directors – just on an intention or a statement, without having a full script.

JM If you have a body of work, you see what people have done before, and can discuss the project. I think that's a normal way. But that is not how it works here. It didn't matter with Channel 4 if you'd made something. Each time you really started at the bottom. I found it got harder by the time we were into the 1990s – it was a very hard period for cultural film-making of any kind. If you look back to the 1970s – I'm not talking just about structural materialist film or avant-garde – there was a lot of stuff being made in Britain, some really great works, and now there isn't. There's hardly been anything going on for 30 years. They killed their own culture. I think the British hate culture.

LC How did Jarman accept the financial control of his projects? For the big productions, he had to deal with other people's desires. Did he have a different artistic approach depending on whether he was working on the big productions or on his independent projects?

JM That was always a problem. Of course, the bigger the project, the more difficult it becomes to shield yourself from the outside. In some projects, such as *The Last of England* and *Blue*, we were able to not have any outside influence at all. Other films were commissions that Derek was engaged on, and the funders or the financers expected a certain thing, and would ask for changes. It's quite common in film-making and commercial film-making for the financers to ask for changes and to interfere with casting and all of that stuff. Fortunately, with films like *The Angelic Conversation*, *The Last of England*, *The Garden*, even in *Blue*, we were totally removed from the thoughts and opinions of others. There's nothing worse than someone's opinion. We did ask people – Derek and I were not completely insular. We did bring people in to look at the work in progress, but they were people who were interested in it. I'm sure that all artists show their work to some extent to people that they confide in, and ask for advice or opinions. But that's constructive criticism. All Derek's films were very modestly funded; the biggest production was around £800,000. That was about a third of the average small film. But he didn't let that stop him realising his ideas. Derek just found different ways to do it.

LC It was not his choice to make do with less money.

JM He'd rather do it than not do it. He just wanted to know how much money was available, and then he'd plan the work knowing that. He didn't say: 'No, I must have a cruise liner and an aeroplane.' He didn't have that blue sky thinking. They weren't constraints, they were just part of the formula. I try to explain that to a lot of younger people working on moving image and film. It's much better to look at what's possible, and to create within that, rather than have an idea for a project that will probably never get made because it's too expensive.

LC That can lead to a lot of sadness and frustration. It seems that Jarman always worked with joy, and tried to pass it on to the people who worked with him. He made the process fun. You spoke of a 'social way of making films', both serious and playful.

JM Derek was a positive person. If he wanted to bring you into his project, he engaged with you enthusiastically. Nobody felt that they were just being hired. He tried to keep it a rewarding experience for everyone. Because of the way we were working, without synchronised sound or anything, we worked a much smaller crew than normal. Even the people that came from the industry that we hired in were involved in the making of the film. They were contributing to the project. That was very rewarding. We had very good electricians and set constructors who really became part of the idea, rather than just being told make this or do that.

FILM EXHIBITIONS, PAST AND PRESENT; TECHNICAL PROBLEMS OF PROJECTION IN THE 1980S; EXHIBITIONS AT LE CRÉDAC, LUMA, SERPENTINE AND ATHENS

LC What about the distribution of these Super-8 films? The public was not really interested in these films at the time Jarman was making them.

JM The thing that's important to understand about Super-8 is that quite a few of the different types of camera – Canon, Nizo – had very good optics, and the film itself had very good emulsion. The problem was, once you had the film shot and processed, when you showed it, the projectors were very dim, largely because it is impossible to bring the tungsten light close enough to the tiny frame to make it bright, because it just burns the film. So you have to have fairly low-powered lamps in the projectors. In the late 1970s, we got Xenon Super-8 projectors using Xenon bulbs. They were pretty good, but they were really hot, and if the film stopped it would just burn, big time. It wasn't very satisfactory. A lot of people who saw the films at the time they were made just saw these little images on the screen, maybe a few feet across and fuzzy, not sharp.

LC When digitising, you adopted Jarman's point of view on camera when he made the films, not what people saw at the screenings at the time.

JM Derek was not happy with that aspect of the film. They were so small and puny. He made his films for a big screen, not for a small screen 'up there' as he called it. With digital scanning, you can get much more information from the actual piece of film, and that makes it easier to blow it up to a good size. People say: 'Oh, but that's not what the medium is. The medium should be small and soft.' I think the medium should be what the person who is making a film saw through the camera, not what one part of the process, one little Super-8 projector, did to that image. It should represent the image that Derek saw when he was making and shooting the film. I think that's what we've done.

LC Was it hard to find venues or places to show the films at that time?

JM There weren't many in those days, because you were looking at festivals of experimental film, maybe some small independent cinemas that did screenings of these type of films, art colleges, some museums, cinematheques, the film Co-op and that's it. There were no other places to show them at the time.

LC Museums and cinemas used to show films only once. Today, the audience for artists' film and video works is quite different. The public now wants to see these films at other times, or on other scales. It's a great responsibility for curators and museum directors to find ways to show these films.

JM It's important to have them shown in a way in which they look their best, as for any art object. If you display a statue, you light it in a certain way, you don't just stick it in a room. It's the same with film. That's a problem because there was not great curatorial training when we were showing stuff in the 1980s and in the 1990s. There was no understanding of how moving images work. Because I came from a slightly different area where we were trained about how to project films, I was always surprised how badly museums and institutions would show work in exhibitions. The whole problem, all the way through from the 1970s until the 2000s, was that electronic imaging was developing very fast, especially in the 1980s and 1990s. Institutions were often buying equipment that would then become obsolete within a couple of years. Hopefully now things are much more settled, which allows for institutions and private galleries to have better access to equipment than they did before.

LC Today the ways of showing these films are endless. For instance, for the exhibition at Le Crédac in 2021, Claire Le Restif, in collaboration with Amanda Wilkinson, decided to project the films on medium-format screens, making the images float in space [SEE P. 33, 34, 40–41].

JM I thought that was really good! I don't think it was intentional, but that was how the films were originally shown in Derek's studio, in his warehouse space. He would have been projecting the films in the same space he was making them, and where he was painting and doing his other work. That got closer to the idea of having paintings on the wall and a film projection in the same space – the installation at Le Crédac brilliantly captured that. Personally, apart from certain films like *Blue*, which is made for a black box – that's how it was shown in Le Crédac as well – I think that films, especially more experimental films like the Super-8 films, can be shown either in a black box situation, or in a much more ambient light situation where you can see the actual room. I don't think it's so necessary anymore to set aside a space for gallery or museum screenings, when you have the new latest generation of projectors which can project a very bright image in daylight. You can now project in a room where you can see things and people and chairs. What's interesting about that is that it's much more like the studio situation where Derek was projecting his films when he first made them: he was projecting in his studio, which might have had direct sunlight blocked out by blinds, but in general we could see the room.

LC Just as a curator hangs several paintings together, some curators also show several films together. That's what you did at the inaugural exhibition of the Luma Foundation in 2021. You decided to show three films together, and suddenly there was something that circulated between them.

JM That's right. It becomes like an exhibition of painting. You have more than one image screening at a time and you can move from one to another. But you can still look back and see the previous one.

LC Is that what Isaac Julien did also at the Serpentine Gallery in the exhibition *Derek Jarman: Brutal Beauty* in 2008?[3]

3 The exhibition was conceived, curated and designed as an immersive environment by the artist and film-maker Isaac Julien. It featured several examples of rarely-seen films from the Jarman Super-8 archive, an installation of Jarman's film *Blue* and a selection of his paintings.

JM Isaac does that, but in a much more complex way. In his films he creates image patterns across multiple screens, so they were actually edited in the way that you see them in the gallery. They're synchronised, so they're always the same. They're made to move in a certain way. With Derek's Super-8s, which are all different lengths, he created a 'galaxy' of images, and the relationship between each changes through time.

LC You also experienced this sometimes with Jarman, didn't you?

JM I did one of the earliest experiments. Derek made a series of diary films which are basically all the bits that he didn't use in his other films, and odd fragments. Because they're all collages of bits of film, it happened by chance. That was the title – *It Happened by Chance* (1972–1983). At one point he started cutting them into different lengths, inspired by the cut-ups William Burroughs and Brion Gysin were doing. Some of them are complete little films within the diaries. There are 12 reels. I thought, well, what can you do with this? They're interesting to look at, but not interesting enough to sit still through. I chose five of them for a screening in Athens (Athens School of Fine Arts, 2006) and made each of them into a loop so that when it got to the end, it would start again. Because each reel was a different length, the relationship

Exhibition view, *Portraits dans le temps*, LUMA Arles, Arles, 2021
Exhibition view, *Derek Jarman: Brutal Beauty*, Serpentine Gallery, London, 2008

between the five images changed throughout the course of the day, radically changed. Simon Fisher Turner made a soundtrack which replicated that musically. He created the music track in the gallery, while the audience was watching the films. On the second day he looped that, so the soundtrack is also looped. Simon and Genesis P-Orridge from the band Throbbing Gristle were the first musicians who worked with Derek's Super-8 films. Before them, all the films had music, but it was from commercial records and cassettes, like Tangerine Dream or William Walton or Ravel. Normally the music or sound for a film is fixed in place, but Simon's music and Genesis P-Orridge's music wasn't synchronous. It was just played with the film. I think it's a much more interesting way of making music for films, because if you have a symphony in parts, it always sounds a bit contrived if it's scored tightly to the picture. For instance, in *The Last of England*, there's the use of Edward Elgar's *Land of Hope and Glory* (1902) when you see India and the Raj and all that. Although the picture was edited to the soundtrack, Derek moved the relationship of picture and sound so they were out of sync. It's much more effective because otherwise it just sounds like it's a music video.

Sulphur, 1975

FILM PRESERVATION AND DISTRIBUTION NOWADAYS: DIGITISATION AND A LIVING ARCHIVE

LC Jarman entrusted you with the great responsibility of looking after his Super-8 archive. You have done this with dedication and respect with the precious help of Luma and others.[4]

JM The original project with Derek was to find a way to conserve and keep the films, especially the Super-8 films, and make them available to the public. That was very difficult in the early 1980s because the only way to make copies of the films that were satisfactory was to make blow ups to 16mm. Super-8 printing wasn't very good. And anyway, we didn't want to project them as Super-8 because of the problems with amount of light and sharpness of the image that made the projection image not very strong. As we went through the 1980s and the 1990s, various things happened. Firstly, broadcast video, like television, got much better, and it was possible to transfer Super-8 to broadcast video. That's 625 PAL video, and we used that quite a bit in the late 1980s. Later on, when I was looking after the films myself, the technology moved on yet again, and the idea of scanning images became possible. But even with scanning possible, it was very complicated in its early days because the file size that was produced by scanning Super-8 to 2k was very big. When we were scanning the Super-8 at the beginning of the Luma project, each frame scanned yielded about 75 MB of information. That's an early scan file that was called a DVX file. DVX was a standard format that could be projected, but it involved a lot of computing power, a lot of memory, a lot of RAM, so it was very expensive to show the films when they were in that format. More recently, other high-quality formats have been developed that can be used to project the films, and at the same time use a lot less computing power – like ProRes 444 HQ, and now H.265 2K – which is much smaller (compressed), but of a high visual quality. This is currently the generally accepted standard for gallery shows and things. It's quite a small file size, with very high picture quality, so it's easy to transmit and use. The same happened with the projectors: in the 1980s video projectors were enormous creatures, and they gradually became more

4 The Luma Foundation in Zurich has acquired all of Jarman's Super-8 films (77 in total), for conservation and distribution purposes. It holds all the rights, and is responsible for looking after them and making them available.

compact. In the last ten years we've moved on to laser projectors, which are very bright, very compact, and the prices have come down a lot.

LC How can curators or film programmers deal with this body of work? How has it been treated so far, and how do you think it will be shown in the future?

JM In the past, arranging viewings of the films for curators had always been a bit complicated, but now it's much simpler. We put the films up on the web, and curators can view them for research purposes. The purpose of the Luma archive is to make the work available – it's not just for preserving or conserving work – so that students, researchers, curators, programmers can view and select work and bring it to their public in exhibitions and screenings in many different ways. Access to the whole archive will be in a permanent room at Luma in Arles, a space designed to allow people to sit and call up whatever material they want from the archive of material that's there. The walls and the rest of the room will be used for exhibition, curated screenings and small discussions. It's not just a workstation, it's also a curated programme space. That's what Maja Hoffman calls a 'living archive'. I can't second-guess what that plan is, but it is to make it even more available than just a URL. That will come, but it takes time. We couldn't have done it 15 years ago because of the file size and the equipment that was available, whereas now it's very easy to do what we intend to do with the space.

JARMAN'S LEGACY: BOOKS AND FILMS; *BLUE* ON TOUR

LC What remains to be done to preserve and disseminate Jarman's work?

JM The other film material has to be given a final home because at the moment I'm looking after *Blue* and *The Garden*, and other films like *Imagining October*. I need to find a permanent home for them. The paintings and the collages are looked after by Amanda Wilkinson. I think there's still the issue of Derek's writing to tackle, not the published books, but the many notebooks that he kept throughout his life. I've been talking to some of the interested parties about this. The way into Derek's work is through his writing. That's really a key thing. And the way into Derek's writing is to take his journals and his workbooks – of which there are many, covering all his projects from the early 1960s, maybe even earlier – and to have those scanned properly so that they can be available online to people who are interested in studying and reading them. There have been pages from his journals published in books in the past, but they've been odd pages, used more as illustrations than further study. It struck me when I was looking at an exhibition in London a few years ago – I think it was at the BFI – you see the journals displayed open, a bit like medieval illuminated manuscripts. You can't turn the pages as they're under glass. The journals have to be made more accessible. Derek's other books are very successful commercially, so they will continue to be printed. Most of the feature-length films are available, they're screened on Channel 4 from time to time, which re-acquired the rights to some films.

LC What about the performance of *Blue*, which is still performed in various contexts?

JM There have been many iterations of *Blue* since the early 1990s. Most recently two performance nights were scheduled at the Bourse de Commerce in Paris. One night in French and one in English.[5] For the 30th anniversary of *Blue,* Neil Bartlett, an illustrious theatre director who was a friend of Derek's, directed a series of live performances of *Blue* in May 2023. The four hosts for *BLUE LIVE* were the Brighton Festival, Turner Contemporary in Margate, HOME in Manchester and Tate Modern. It was performed by Russell Tovey, Travis Alabanza, Jay Bernard and Joelle Taylor, with music by Fisher Turner. The future will no doubt yield more performances and gallery installations. There is a dance piece in the pipeline.

5 On 1 and 2 December 2021, two evenings in tribute to Derek Jarman were held in the auditorium of the Bourse de Commerce – Pinault Collection, in partnership with Le Crédac and the Festival d'Automne à Paris. The first evening featured a performance of the complete script of *Blue*, read by artist Lili Reynaud Dewar and actor Yves-Noël Genod, accompanied by musician Simon Fisher Turner and visual artist and musician Rainier Lericolais. The second evening featured a live electronic and experimental performance by Fisher Turner with Swedish composer Klara Lewis, British cellist Lucy Railton and pianist Steve Nieve, accompanied by a free reading of the *Blue* script by Lili Kim and American artist and writer Black Sifichi.

ARTISTIC ASPECTS OF JARMAN'S OEUVRE: NARRATIVE VS. PAINTERLY QUALITIES OF HIS FILMS; MUSIC COLLABORATION; POETRY

LC Can you talk about the difference in Jarman's filmography between his films with a scenario – telling a story, with a narrative – and his other films. Is there a difference in his cinematography between images versus narrative stories? Is that where the difference between a storyteller and a poet lies? The poet creates images or sensations, while a storyteller or an historian or a playwright tells a plain story.

JM There is a tendency to separate what you call the narrative films from the more painterly ones. But I think that many of Derek's films have a kind of narrative or make logical sense. Not all of them – some are very abstract. But even the short Super-8 films have a kind of internal narrative. You've got to understand how Derek entered the world of commercial cinema. His first commercial film, and by commercial I mean the first shown in cinemas, *Sebastiane* (1976), is not a project that Derek developed himself. The film was originally someone else's project. It was meant to be a kind of documentary about Saint Sebastian. I don't know the whole story, because I never really asked Derek about it. All I know is that he got involved in this other version of *Sebastiane* because his project on a similar topic wasn't moving anywhere and this one was. To some extent, there is obviously the narrative, and there's a simple story of Sebastian, but I don't think that was particularly Derek's interest. Making the whole thing in sort of a schoolboy Latin goes against the normal idea of making a narrative documentary or a narrative drama. I don't think Derek was ever very interested in narrative. The idea of a script was really forced on him because that was the only way that he could raise funds for bigger films. He was not trained as a script writer and it took him a long time to write a script. It often involved many other people. Films like *The Tempest* and *Edward II* (1991) essentially have a script that was already written, which Derek then adapted. He'd work with other people to adapt it because he was much more interested in the image. The same

Derek Jarman showering Leonardo Treviglio on the set of *Sebastiane*, 1976

is true of *Wittgenstein* (1993), which already came with a completed script by Terry Eagleton. Derek wasn't really that interested in the script, he was much more interested in Wittgenstein's ideas. He always just deconstructed. If there was a narrative, he deconstructed it, and then he reassembled it as a series of images that create meaning in the progress of the sequences, one against the other. He spoke about feature films as being made up of approximately 32 sequences rather than a three-act drama. That's how he ended up working in a format. I don't mean a format in terms of film gauge. I mean a format of conventional commercial cinema. That really wasn't what he was interested in. At the time when Derek was working, there was no real space for an ambitious artist's moving image work. There were examples like Sergei Parajanov and others through the history of cinema. But cinema is very much guided by commerce. The audience wants story, and that's a kind of convention – the one that makes money, so it's been the dominant form. There are lots of other ways to use film. Derek started off making films that he wanted to make. They weren't films that other people made. By working in Super-8, a very small format, Derek was limiting the size of the audience. To get a bigger audience and a bigger image, first of all he migrated to 16mm with *Sebastiane, Jubilee* and *The Tempest*, and then to 35mm. But he wanted to use it in a different way. In fact, after he made *Edward II* in 35mm, he was very pleased that he'd found the method of making *Edward II* closer to the way that he made the Super-8 films. If you look at *Edward II* again, it's a series of sequences rather than a narrative. When Derek was in hospital, the second director took over, and suddenly you've got reverse cutting, reverse-field shots, which just don't exist in Derek's other films. Derek never used those tools of conventional narrative cinema.

LC You said Derek was looking for meaning, but not for narrative.

JM It's the same way that a painting that gives you a satisfactory meaning, conveying ideas or discourse without necessarily being figurative. Similarly, a film doesn't have to be narrative, it doesn't have to be talking heads. I always felt, and I think Derek felt it as well, that a cinema of talking heads is very limited. Radio with pictures.

LC Jarman was also involved in producing images for music. When he was making music videos, he was at the other end of the chain. He had the music and had to add images to it. But he wasn't just putting images to the music. He was doing something different.

JM The music videos are really a different thing. Some of them are rather good, like The Smiths' *The Queen Is Dead* (1986) because it's much more like a film than it is a music promo. But they were largely commercial work. We needed the money, basically. Although the music and the musicians we worked for were very good, Derek didn't see it as being serious work. It bordered on it at times, in certain areas. It was interesting, but it was a means to an end. The musicians and the public got something good. I think it also changed the way that music videos were made at a certain point, although that's not very recognised. When people do the history of music videos, they ignore The Smiths and stuff like that. After we made *The Queen Is Dead*, people started doing these really fast cutting things. A little bit later, we made the Pet Shop Boys' *It's a Sin* (1987), which is really kind of classic, with no fades or any kind of effect. You could do something different to what everybody else was doing at the time.

LC Music is the only art that Derek didn't try.

JM He did! Derek played the musical saw. He wasn't very good at it. I think he probably just chose the wrong instrument. Maybe he should have chosen a Theremin. He'd have been so happy. The musical saw is very difficult to master. He liked music very much and he had a wide taste and interest in music. He worked with many musicians. We mentioned Simon and Genesis, but there was also Marianne Faithfull and Diamanda Galás. Diamanda provided the music for the end of *The Last of England*. There were many others.

LC Poetry was also a major axis of Jarman's work.

JM He wrote poetry before he made films. I assumed that was a more natural medium for him than film-making. But I'm more familiar with the poetry that appears later in the films, especially in *The Garden* and then in *Blue*, than I am with his earlier poetry, which I think he abandoned a bit in the wake of *A Finger in the Fishes Mouth* (1972), which wasn't very successful when he published it. Maybe he decided that wasn't a good direction to follow. He only really revived writing poetry after *The Angelic Conversation*; I think that by using the Shakespeare sonnets in the film, he probably saw that he could use his poetry in a film as well.

LC Many of his writings are pieces of poetry in themselves. I'm thinking of *Chroma* (1994).

JM That came later. Before *The Angelic Conversation*, there wasn't a lot of writing. The first major piece of writing is *Dancing Ledge* (1984), which I still think is his best book by far. The structure of it is really interesting and it gives you almost a cubist picture of Derek's life, where you catch different facets of it, rather than just seeing it as one linear thread.

ANALYSIS OF JARMAN'S OEUVRE: RECURRING MOTIFS; MYSTICISM; EFFECTS; MIRRORS

LC Could we talk a little more about some of Jarman's motifs? For instance, the motif of the bed. It keeps coming back in his films, and in his installations as well. Is it a chaste metaphor for sex? What does it tell us about intimacy?

JM I think it's probably better to start at the beginning and to speak about motifs in general. When I first started to see Derek's work, one thing that I noticed was that he used recurring motifs. There were people and objects that would reappear in different works. There were ways of costuming and designing the figures in his films. That was quite apparent early on. Like the use of the paper bag as a mask – that was very frequent when I met Derek. Then there was the use of various kinds of makeup, sometimes to move noses or to change things, but often the same use for different people. Then there was the use of objects, anything from statues to jewellery. He had a collection of things in his small apartment. Like a plaster head that was a cast of a figure on top of the tower of St George's Church in Bloomsbury in London, designed by Nicholas Hawksmoor and consecrated in 1730. Derek thought it was the head of a Roman emperor, when in fact it was King George I in Roman costume, but no matter! This plaster cast had been part of the Slade archive, plaster casts of classical works that the students would use for sketching. They were throwing them out when Derek arrived at the Slade, so he picked up a few of them. This head appears in a lot of Derek's films and works. The use of motifs through objects, or re-casting the same people in different parts was very strong from the beginning. In the films from the period when he became HIV-positive, the motif of the bed became very important, his hospital bed. It appears quite often in installations, paintings, films of the time. So do other things, especially in the later paintings. In his late period, the collages have a lot of religious and medical objects, and of course, mirrors. In his early Super-8s, mirrors reflect the sun, in the paintings there is broken mirror, and it's the same mirror, really. People would say about some of the Super-8s, like the series of *In the Shadow of the Sun*: 'They all look a bit the same.' But Monet's haystacks also all look a bit the same, but they're not the same. They're all different ways of looking at the same image, but treating it in different ways. That, of course, is a painterly concern rather than a narrative filmmaker's concern.

Bed (IV), 1988–1989
Bed (VII), 1988–1989

LC Brilliantly put! I will come back to the bed. There is a very interesting way of using the bed in the video clip for Orange Juice, *What Presence?!* (1984), where a man sleepwalks down the street in his bed.

JM Yes, Derek had seen that in a carnival, somebody looked like he was sleeping in a bed, so he had that copied. Of course, it must have impressed him because it was a bed.

LC Sometimes it's only one person in the bed, like Jarman in *The Garden*, alone in the bed in the sea. But often there are two people in the bed. Both in his films, and in his exhibition at the Third Eye Centre in Glasgow (1989), where a bed with two people – surrounded by large-scale bed installations, in which mattresses were scattered with books – stood in the middle of the gallery. That brings in something very delicate, very tender.

JM In *Jubilee*, there's the mattress with the two brothers.

LC In Jarman's Bankside studio the bed was also in the middle of the room, under a greenhouse made of plastic. It looked as if bed was at the centre of his life, or at least had a very important place in it.

JM I suppose you could say that. In his Phoenix House flat in Charing Cross Road the bedroom was his living room and vice versa. The bed was just a mattress on the floor where people would sit. Then that was replaced by a formal grand oak bed made for Derek by Andy Marshall. The reason for the greenhouse in the studio at Bankside was because it was so cold. Derek lived in such small spaces that the bed was often in the middle.

LC What about the mystical aspects of Jarman's work? The holy dimension, rituals, everything related to religion. He made his own religious ornaments, like icons and reliquaries, a personal, cobbled-together religiosity. He rejected priests and the Anglican church. It seems that his relationship to the holy was complex.

JM When I first met him, he was very interested in mysticism, in the work of John Dee[6] and others. He studied that quite thoroughly, because that was also the period of history that he studied at university. He collected books and objects on that period. He was very knowledgeable about it. Derek was very interested in that and other forms of ritual magic, but not the sort of the fancy dress stuff, the serious stuff. He practiced esotericism as a person. If he was making a film, he would draw the circle. He did that for every film, it was set up like a spell so that the film existed within the circle. And there were people in the circle and people outside the circle.

6 John Dee (1527–1608) was an English mathematician, astronomer, astrologer, teacher, occultist and alchemist. He was an advisor to Elizabeth I. He had one of the largest libraries in England at the time. As a political advisor, he advocated the foundation of English colonies in the New World to form a 'British Empire' a term he is credited with coining. Because he was a mystic and spoke to the angels – he wrote *The Angelic Conversation* – the Church did not favour him although he was Christian in faith.

LC Do you mean metaphorically or on the set?

JM I mean really, in his private apartment, while preparing the film. He was very much involved in that. He told me before he died that he had broken his wound, which signifies letting go of your worldly powers. I'm not that familiar with all those aspects of Dee's magic. But Derek was, and it influenced all of his films very deeply, especially *The Tempest*, of course, which would have been influenced by Dee anyway because it was written following Elizabeth I. Prospero, the island, etc., the whole thing is a metaphor for arcane knowledge. Shakespeare doesn't say what the books that Prospero takes to the island are, but the people who study Dee and Shakespeare know what the books are. Derek certainly seemed to think that he knew what the books were. He said that's the difference between him and Greenaway: 'Peter doesn't know what books Prospero took to the island, I do.' And, of course, *In the Shadow of the Sun*, that's another thing from that philosophy, the sun comes with shadow. And 'Silence is Golden', a phrase Derek often uses, also comes from Dee.

Studio Bankside, 1972

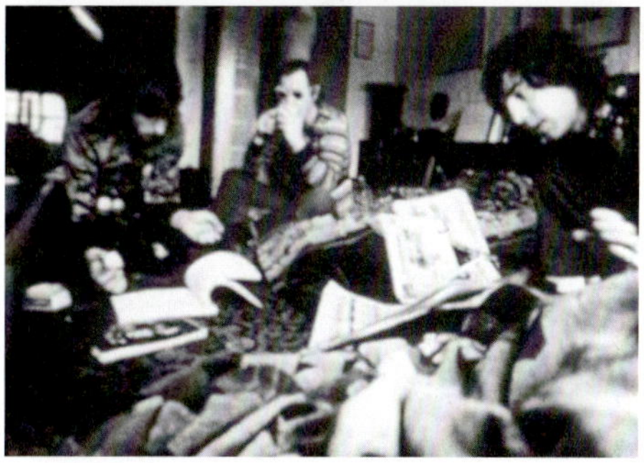

LC As we are talking about the regular motifs that keep coming back into Jarman's movies, there are also ways of filming that recur in his filmography, such as slowing down the image, superimposition and the use of colour filters.

JM It comes in different phases. Some of the early Super-8 films use colour filters, like *Journey to Avebury* (1973) that was filmed using a yellow filter, and *Red Movie* (1973), with a red filter. But they use very straightforward cutting. The frame rate of those films is 18 frames a second, which is the normal speed of the camera and the projector. Then there's a second phase that leads up to *In the Shadow of the Sun*, where he started to superimpose images, and change the speed of the projection of the images while he was filming. That ends around about 1974 with *In the Shadow of the Sun* and *Sulphur* (1975). Later, there's a different kind of filming at a very low speed, six frames a second, which is then projected at a lower speed. There are definitely periods of different techniques in Derek's work, much as a painter would have: they change, they modify, they learn, they get interested in new aspects of the process.

LC Which marks his style and his signature as well.

JM I think so. He explored film creatively, as opposed to somebody who is interested in drama, who would just treat the film camera as a machine that simply recorded what they were putting in front of it. Derek used the process of filming as part of the art.

LC Tilda Swinton pointed out that most of the figures and the heroes in Jarman's films were some aspect of himself. When he chose Caravaggio or Wittgenstein, it was himself that he was depicting.

JM Before he died, he told me quite clearly that all the central characters in his films, all the protagonists from Prospero to Sebastian, were expressions of himself. *Blue* was himself as well, but not in the disguise of a character. It was the first time that he had openly expressed himself through his film.

LC In this sense his use of mirrors could be seen as mirrors of himself?

JM In a way, yes. Mirrors of reality and distortions of reality. A key film for Derek, the one that probably influenced him most strongly, was *The Testament of Orpheus* (1960) by Jean Cocteau. In that film in particular there is a magical relationship between poetry and cinema, and that's what Derek was interested in.

LC If Cocteau can be considered one of his mentors, do you see Jarman as a mentor to the younger generation?

JM Oh, yes. Lots of people take his courage and his way of looking at the medium as their starting point. Younger people are influenced by him, but obviously they might be influenced by other people as well. There isn't a school of Derek Jarman. I remember I had a conversation with Liam Gillick who said that when he was a student he was very influenced by Derek's more experimental films, which I think is really interesting. He didn't have much of an influence on his contemporaries, but one or two of them, such Sally Potter and Ron Peck, work a kind of cross influence. Jarman has definitely had an influence on the younger generation.

Tarot (The Magician), 1973

JARMAN AND HIS POLITICAL SIDE

LC My next question is about political aspect of Jarman.

JM I'll tell you all I know about Derek politically. When I first met him, he was very friendly with Vanessa Redgrave, who he knew from *The Devils*. She was part of a Trotskyite group called the Workers Revolutionary Party (WRP). She recruited Derek to go leafletting and on marches. He canvased the council estates handing out WRP leaflets with Vanessa. He said it was amazing. One time they were in a block of working-class apartments, and they knocked on the door, a man came, looked at them, turned around and shouted to his wife: 'It's that bloody Vanessa!' He wanted to support Vanessa and the cause, but he was not a political animal, not at all at that time. I filmed an interview for Luma with Genesis P-Orridge before they died, and they talked about when they met Derek during the gay liberation meetings in the late 1960s, early 1970s. They were both involved with that, but I think, like Genesis, Derek left once it became part of a wider political concern that had moved away from being a drive for equality into other areas of politics. He joined the gay liberation meetings to fight for gay liberation, but when it became about other causes and other political things, a lot of people that were involved left, because they weren't particularly interested in wider political issues. Once it lost its focus, he didn't think it was going to achieve its goal, because it became very diffuse. People were looking at lots of other things that they felt needed to change. He only really got politicised again when he first got ill with HIV (although he made a number of interventions in the debates around film funding). He got involved with ACT UP, which was a really interesting group of people. ACT UP was fun because it was quite hectic. It had lots of different kinds of people in it from lots of different walks of life, and it was very open. Then obviously things changed there as well and it became fractionalised politics and you also got Stonewall (1969) and all those things, which now seem to be maybe not as useful as they were at the time. Derek was always a supporter of simple agitation for change, but he didn't like the complex stuff when it got bogged down in political manoeuvring.

Journey to Avebury, 1973

LC In his fight for the recognition of HIV/AIDS patients, he used his name and fame.

JM Yes, he was one of the first people to come out as being HIV-positive in 1987, so that was a huge thing. The nature of his work incorporated his life into it in many ways. Derek wasn't a politician; he wasn't a political animal who had a political agenda.

LC He was living politically because he never hid that he was gay and HIV-positive.

JM That's a personal politics. You live your life as you are. Other people who shall be nameless were doing the same thing, but they had another agenda maybe. I don't think Derek had an agenda. He just wanted to get on with his life and make his films and hope that his work would change things, but not in a way that forced people to change. He wanted them to find a way to change within themselves.

LC And shine a new light on problems or issues.

JM To look at history and to see how things have always been. If you look at gay life or at what's called queer life, it happens throughout history, and it has resulted in lots of great things. Derek just wanted people to see that, as opposed to the negativity that was being presented by the government in Section 28,[7] and that whole struggle. He didn't want to get involved as a politician. He was very worried about people who became political and then accepted honours from the Queen. Derek never looked for honours.

LC Dungeness and Margate are now places where refugees arrive in England from Calais. I always wonder how Jarman would have reacted to these crucial social issues of today. I have read that some people in the community of Dungeness are now involved in welcoming refugees who arrive on the coast.

JM Personally, I don't know very much about Dungeness today. But, I think it's in the films, isn't it? At the end of *The Last of England*, the refugees are leaving on their boat and in *The Garden* they've arrived in this place.

LC Derek joined the two movies?

JM They were sequential, the two films join up. At least that's what Derek imagined when we began making *The Garden*. *The Garden* follows *The Last of England* as he was thinking about what happened to the people who left in the boat at the end of the film. Where did they go to? In the painting *The Last of England* (1855) by Ford Maddox Brown, two emigrants leave England to start a new life in Australia with their baby.[8] The film is directly related to the painting: you can see the cabbages that are in the painting. The scene where the refugees are huddled on the edge of the dock getting ready to leave was very influenced by the painting as well.

LC What about *The Garden*?

JM *The Garden* is the Garden of Eden, so they arrived from their journey in the boat to a place of shingle, which is the Garden of Eden, or Gethsemane, or the Garden of Earthly

7 Section 28 or Clause 28 was a legislative designation for a series of laws across Britain that prohibited the 'promotion of homosexuality' by local authorities. Introduced by Margaret Thatcher's Conservative government, it was in effect from 1988 to 2000 in Scotland and from 1988 to 2003 in England and Wales.

8 Ford Maddox Brown, *The Last of England*, 1855. Two finished versions of the picture exist, one in Birmingham Museum and Art Gallery, and the other one in the Fitzwilliam Museum in Cambridge.

Delights. That was a key idea there. Just as the *Black Paintings* (1819–1823) by Goya were a key to *The Last of England*, so those references were to *The Garden*.

LC This question about refugees today in Dungeness is also a way of summoning Jarman's presence in the 2020s. As with many people who died in the 1980s and 1990s from HIV, we try to imagine life and the world today with these people still alive. Do you ever think about that in terms of Jarman? Do you think about what he would be like, what he would be doing today?

JM I'm sure he would be very proactive in helping people off the beach. Of course, he would be outraged. Yes, he was outraged about people being treated badly.

Derek Jarman with a cast of his face made by Christopher Hobbs, 1980

SUPER-8 FILMS 1972–1976

Three Super-8 films exhibited in *Derek Jarman. Dead Souls Whisper (1986–1993)*, Centre d'art contemporain d'Ivry – le Crédac, Ivry-sur-Seine, 2021.

Death Dance, 1973

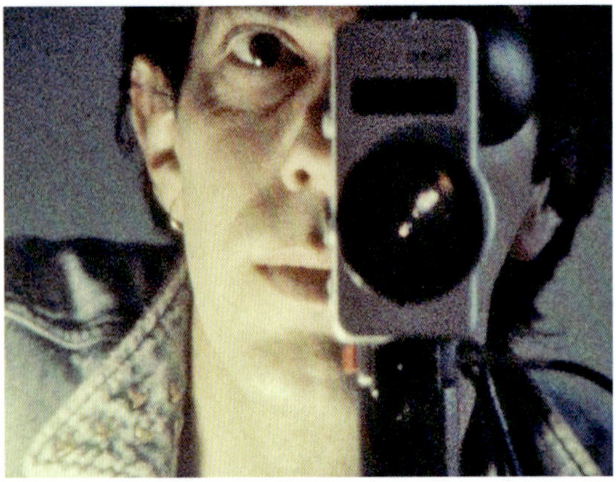

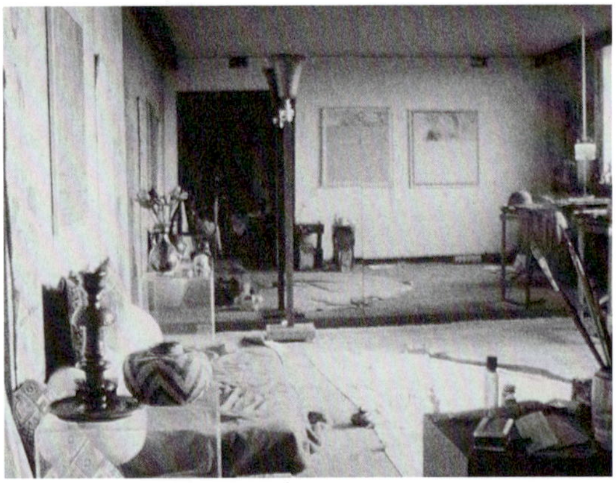

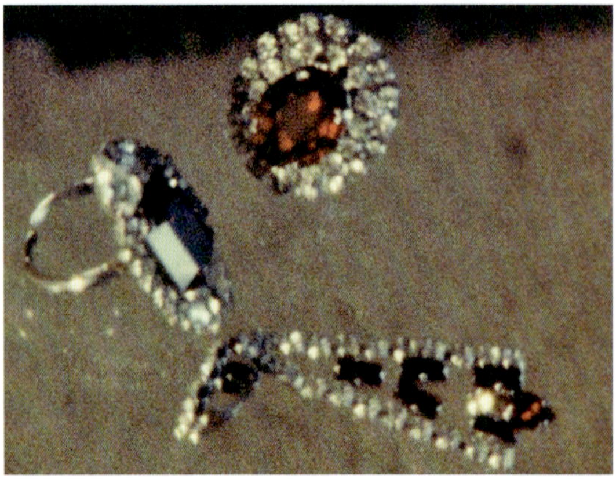

At Low Tide, 1972

TESTIMONIALS

TIME AND TIDE PHILIP HOARE

* This contribution by Philip Hoare is a modified version of his text first published in *INQUE Magazine*, 2023, p. 50–52.

On steady, luminous Super-8 film shot on a hot summer's day on an English shore, the sea runs out at low tide, leaving behind a drowned sailor in a rockpool, stripped half-naked by the sea, his blond hair waving like weeds [*At Low Tide*, 1972]. The long-haired siren who lured him there perches on a rock, wearing only a fishing net wrapped around her slender body.

On the cliff above, a sea god appears in a glittering silver mask with golden eyes and a multicoloured robe seemingly made from seaweed, seawater and clouds. He descends to wrap his arms around the siren, as if to still her voice. As the last frame spools out, the mask and robe are left on the rocks, washed by the sea.

All this is silent. All this in a magical seven minutes, a moment lost in wonder; in a strange, innocent, debauched time. It is a memory of something I never knew. The impossible dreams of teenage years, all that striving for transformation and change, all caught up in a film I would not see for another five decades. Half a century stands between me now and it then, in the flickering fallback of time.

In 1972, Derek Jarman was living in a semi-derelict, 19th-century warehouse on the Thames in London, where he slept in a greenhouse he had put up for shelter inside the cavernous building. From the doors that opened onto the water he could watch the river go by, swelling brown and fast along the deserted South Bank. Jarman was then known as an artist and a designer, not yet as a film-maker. But here, two years previously, in 1970, he had met a young American who would change the course of his art.

Marc Balet was an architectural student at the prestigious Rhode Island School of Design in New England; he had been studying in Rome and had come to London in search of a job. Balet had a new toy: a Super-8 cine camera. He showed it to Jarman, who was intrigued. Jarman borrowed it to make his first films, shooting around his loft and recording his friends, key members of the world of art and fashion that linked the more louche ends of the 1960s with the new, as-yet-unnamed movements of the 1970s.

It was a camp, kitsch aesthetic, highly self-referential and hermetic, spinning off from David Hockney's avowedly gay sensibility, and about to emerge publicly in the invented personae of David Bowie and Roxy Music. All would draw deeply on this group of artists and extroverts who Peter York would call 'Them'.

'They' were a 'mysterious aesthetic conspiracy', as York put it, and their ranks included Andrew Logan, the artist who, in 1972, would stage their defining event: the first outrageous travesty of his Alternative Miss World in his Hackney studio. Then there was Duggie Fields, whose 1950s-influenced pop art relocated that decade as a fantasy version of itself; Chelita Secunda, the stylist who had almost singlehandedly launched 'glam rock' (a phrase neither she nor her peers would use) by swiping glitter under Marc Bolan's eyes before he went on Top of the Pops; Luciana Martínez de la Rosa, artist and muse of Kevin Whitney, whose obsession with beautiful athletes' bodies led him to become the official Olympic artist; and Ulla Larson-Styles, a Swedish actor, model and wild child who, in 1974, would be arrested for trying to liberate a chandelier from Harrods by tying it under her voluminous skirt.

Jarman, handsome and having recently come to terms with his own sexuality, found a natural home with such hedonists, and they found an immortalist in him. Much as with Warhol's Factory superstars, they became the cast and co-creators of Jarman's films: sharp, edited glimpses of anarchic, self-consciously glamorous lives – performers resisting the drabness, the oppressions, the signs of their times.

July 1972: Jarman proposes a road trip to make a new film. The location will be in Dorset, the 'twilit England' he remembered from childhood holidays. Christopher Hobbs has made the props – a 'mask of genius' and dozens of silver paper boats. Balet will be the cinematographer. It will star Logan, who has brought his own costume, along with his wind-up gramophone (Logan tells me he often travelled with it). Also on board are a handsome young Danish couple, architectural students named Ernst and Bente Lohse, and an anonymous young man called Ian.

They drive down in an old car, passing Corfe Castle, which guards the Isle of Purbeck – where coincidentally I saw my first dolphin during a family trip in the summer of 1972 – and on to the coast at Winspit, where an abandoned quarry has left caverns honeycombing the cliffs. But what seemed like a good idea evaporates in the dark and the damp and the discomfort of the reality. Their foam bed is useless against hard limestone, and they eat their cold supper in a state of misery.

Not even the sound of *Land of Hope and Glory* on Logan's gramophone can raise their spirits. Stormy weather rages outside, as if the scenario were turning into Shakespeare's *The Tempest*. And despite a ritual dose of Valium doled out by Balet, who receives a monthly supply from his mother in Connecticut, the magic deserts them. They sleep fitfully and awake bleary-eyed to discover that the location for their film – the rocks and surging sea below – has completely disappeared into the rain and the fog.

To make amends, Jarman suggests that they take shelter not far away in a Jacobean manor house owned by a friend of his, Michael Pinney. Earlier that year, Pinney had published the first book of Jarman's poems in a provocative edition with a Willem von Gloden photograph of a naked Sicilian youth on the cover [*A Finger in the Fishes Mouth*, 1972]. The well-worn brick and limestone house, nestled in the valley, has been in his family since they built it in 1694. Jarman is clearly hoping to impress his American and Danish friends with such historical charms. And Pinney cooperates by inviting his friends, the artists Reynolds and Janet Stone, as well as the writer John Bailey and his wife, Iris Murdoch.

Jarman's film would have hardly sounded surprising or far-fetched to Murdoch; perhaps the two artists even saw echoes of their characters in each other. Like Murdoch, Jarman had long been obsessed with the magical themes of *The Tempest*, and would later film it, too, having tried to engage Bowie to sing the part of the shape-shifting spirit Ariel.

Late that night, Jarman and his friends drive all the way back to London, defeated in their attempt to make their film. They leave the Isle of Purbeck behind them, vanishing into the mist.

At Low Tide, 1972

Jarman and his friends return to Winspit on the hottest day of the year. They act out their shadow play.

'My robe was the robe for the Alternative Miss World 1972', Logan recalls. He perches on top of the cliff. The camera, operated by Balet as an extension of Jarman's eye, picks out a spiky trawler passing by. Its black shape, its rigging and nets, are followed by a cloud of gulls. Then the lens steadily ranges up the rocky cliffs to find the sea god standing there.

Logan is wearing his helmet-mask of genius, made from scored and folded silver cardstock. Logan's arms are full of his cloak-robe-dress. He's half naked and skinny, his voluminous white pantaloons like sails held up by braces. Standing on the cliff, masked and gowned, his down-stretched hand points to the sea lapping in, and the shallow rockpool in which a young man lies, all washed up. He might have fallen from the sun, like Icarus in Herbert Draper's lavish painting of 1898.

The siren sits on the rock, looking out to sea, her long legs folded to one side; Bente is assuming, almost automatically, the pose of the Little Mermaid from her native Copenhagen. She's unadorned, clad only in her long blonde hair and a green fishing net wrapped around her. She folds silver boats and floats them in the pool. There's something Shelleyan about all this slow-motion anarchy and its masks: the world turned upside-down. The whole thing was very symbolic, says Balet. 'It was totally Derek's idea', he says. The working title was *The Siren and the Sailor*. Later it became known as *At Low Tide*, which is odd, since it is clear that the sea is most definitely at high tide.

The sailor lies behind Bente in the pool: her victim, he is stripped to the waist; he is beautiful, untouched flotsam, swaying in the sun; Eliot's drowned Phoenician sailor turned up by a tarot card. His white bell-bottom duck trousers are worthy of Herman Melville's handsome sailor, Billy Budd; but the buttons at his waist are bright orange, with 1970s allure, and he lacks a Charles Atlas body, as Jarman would say. No one thought pumped-up muscles desirable then.

As the siren floats the little silver foil boats, the sea god picks his way over the rocks like a Technicolor cormorant. He stalks past the dead sailor and embraces the siren.

Comforting her in her grief as she mourns the sailor, silencing her song. His rags close around her till we see her no more. In the last frame, we see the god's mask and gown splayed out on the rocks like the skin of a selkie; the waves appear to be about to drag them into the sea.

And there the film ends. Nothing really happens. Nothing is resolved, everything is suggested. Jarman and his friends spend the rest of the day sunbathing. Fifty years ago.

In the time between then and now, the Lohses went on to become architect stars of Scandinavian design, celebrated in Denmark and beyond. Balet became the editor of Andy Warhol's *Interview* magazine. Logan has established a museum of his own work in Wales and continued to stage his Alternative Miss Worlds until 2008. And Ian, despite my own and others' best efforts, faded into anonymity.

Jarman, had he survived the HIV infection which took his life in 1994, would now be in his 80s, enjoying the glory of recent retrospective exhibitions of his work in Dublin, Manchester, Ivry-sur-Seine and Southampton. Looking back, with some trepidation, his short films from the 1970s seem much less like curtain-raisers to his later, full-length works – such as *Sebastiane*, *Jubilee*, *The Tempest*, *Caravaggio* and *The Garden* – than like precise aesthetic experiments, extended acts of retrieval. They link the neo-romantic, apocalyptic art of Jarman's creative inheritance – the 1940s and 1950s films of Michael Powell and Emeric Pressburger, the paintings of Paul Nash, John Minton and Keith Vaughan – with the glitter and darkness of the early 1970s and their sense of possibilities and disruptions, of new identities.

Those short films show the traces of a highly refined style that was already appearing in the work of Bowie and Roxy Music. Bryan Ferry's sea-fantasy for Roxy Music's blue-tinted *Siren* cover (1975), in which a mermaid-like Jerry Hall crawls out of the sea onto the rocks, seems to combine *At Low Tide* with *Corfe Film* (1975), another short made in Dorset by Jarman featuring Martínez as a pearl-draped Pre-Raphaelite maiden filmed through a blue gel.

But it is the analogue, almost fugitive power of those works that speaks to us now. Jarman spoke of 'the pleasure of Super-8 films as seeing language put through magic lanterns; you don't know what you have to say until you've said it. You can dream of lands far distant.' His short films, embedded in celluloid like stained glass and made for their own sake, stand in contrast to the digital speed of our 21st-century culture. In their ghostly slowness they connect us physically with that fluid age of change and possibilities. As Prospero asks Miranda, his daughter, 'What seest thou else / In the dark backward and abyss of time?'

May 1976: That mask left behind on the rocks? I might have picked it up and put it on. That spring, I saw the Starman on stage. He threw a lover's dart in my eyes and quoted Prospero's words about woven dreams and one magical moment. It was a ducal command, delivered in the black-and-white guise of Man Ray and the Velvet Underground. As I came out of the auditorium, I saw a pair of extraordinarily-dressed people in lurex and PVC, who I would only later recognise from the *New Musical Express* as Siouxsie Sioux and Steve Severin. They were a new mythic cast, crawling out of the suburbs.

That autumn, I went to college in outer London, and took the train into the centre of the city at night, queuing up in a no-man's land devoid of shops – Covent Garden – where a boy in a black leather jacket with peroxided hair asked me for a light. Then I descended into the basement of the Roxy Club and everything changed.

A year later, a friend showed me the script of a new film that was being made, and said I could be an extra in it if I liked. I read the script and thought it was ridiculous – I turned down the offer. The film was Jarman's *Jubilee*.

April 2022: The sun breaks through as we stumble down to the cove. The caves open up like letterboxes in the cliffs. The sea roars in below. It's a treacherous place. One Valium-sedated misstep after midnight and that would have been the end of a great career. The caves are covered in graffiti dating back to the 1960s, stones carved by the stoned. We climb down to the wave-washed ledge, studded with shrunken sea anemones like spat-out sweets, and slithery, treacherous seaweed in green and pink.

By the miracle of five decades' advance, a satellite of love beams down the moving image. The silent film rolls out on K's phone. The sea supplies the soundtrack it never had. We work out where the sailor washed up, where the siren sat, where the god descended from the sky. The tide is coming in. Soon it will be high. The gulls wheel over our heads.

The film spins to an end, and we get ready to get in.

WE WERE COCKY
GERALD INCANDELA

Helmut Berger was not coming out of his bedroom. The eight or so of us were waiting in his big sparse white living room to go out to dinner. I was dancing with a young woman with short hair and someone else to Elton John's *Honky Cat* (1972). Apparently nobody knew who that woman was and what she was doing there. I still don't get it. Jay, one of the Johnson twins, was also there that night, but I didn't know who he was at the time. Certain looks you don't forget!

That night in Rome I heard Derek Jarman's name for the first time. I don't remember who announced with great excitement that this cutting-edge English set designer was in Rome for a Ken Russell movie project, nor do I remember meeting Derek very soon thereafter, more than likely at the apartment of Nando Scarfiotti who had a functioning bathtub on his roof terrace above the via dei Condotti. Nando had been the production designer for Luchino Visconti's *Death in Venice* (1971); he was handsome, kind and perfect in everything he did or said. His approval of another 'style maker' meant everything in our clique.

Derek was travelling with Patrick Steede; I remember him telling me in Nando's living room that they were doing their own research on the side, for a script on Saint Sebastian. I see Patrick laughing as he said he was going to write it in Latin, but he was one of those bright English characters who would never commit to anything, and therefore never wrote a line. There have been other Patricks in Derek's life. No names.

My first memory of Derek is in a bathtub, two weeks later, in a penthouse full of blue and white porcelain, expat style, belonging to one of his friends. I am sure I remember that moment because I think this is where the question was popped. I also remember him in my dark basement apartment when he suggested that I follow him to London. Odd that I don't remember any romantic or sexual moment, only the smell of Pears soap. On the other hand, I do remember the feeling of having found a protector in Derek. He was concerned by my hash habit at the time, in a country where being caught would land one in jail for years, as happened to the unfortunate actor Pierre Clementi. His message came through and I had to decide. I had come to Rome to play a tiny part in a movie with the sublime actress Silvana Mangano, and was hanging out with directors and actresses. I was 21, and realised when the lights and camera focused on me that I was self-conscious in a bad way. I was never going to be an actor. Still, I was driven to go somewhere without knowing where yet. So when Derek proposed London, I said okay, and three weeks after meeting him for the first time, following a quick affair with Patrick, we were, the three of us, on a plane heading to England.

Fifty years ago, romance and marriage were not 'in' generally; friendship was. Bette Midler's song *Friends* (1972) became comfort food to many single people. In those years of disco and sex one would risk being perceived as needy by falling in love for more than one night. Sex was the fashionable sport then, and Derek practiced at night in public parks where, I imagine, he went for sex, and, because he loved to walk through the architecture of London's empty streets at night, I am sure he liked to observe the characters he would come across. A pub in plein air where you cut to the chase and didn't spend any money. I never went. Once he did take me to an apartment where several men had gathered for sex. Had any of it had been tasteful in any way, I might have stayed.

It's very odd now to remember that I didn't mind his night adventures nor did any of the others who followed me. I never met Keith Collins, Derek's last partner, so he is not included in this early group. To his credit, Derek created an atmosphere that spared us the ugliness of possessiveness. All of us boyfriends were in our early 20s and were part of his art making in some way.

He was not a mentor, but he gave us a chance before anybody else would if he thought we had talent or were just smart. This quality must have been very useful in giving confidence to his actors! He didn't seem to be jealous, having made a movie of me making love, through a red filter, with someone he produced out of thin air and I never saw again. Had I been willing bait? On the other hand, I still don't understand why he wrote that I left in tears

Gerald Incandela in *Art & the Pose*, 1977

when I moved out his Sloane Square apartment. I had happily fallen in love and was surprised that he took it badly. I didn't expect this pride, or had I missed something? We survived the breakup, and he unwittingly got his revenge when he introduced me to the famous collector Sam Wagstaff, who eventually whisked me away to the States, ending the three-year relationship for which I had left Derek.

But back to London and Derek's boyfriends: we were all good friends and we often ganged up on Derek because he was fun to tease. We were all too young to separate the man we knew, as intimately as Britain allows, from his work. We were cocky and did not take his work very seriously at the time.

Was it because he would get so excited during his Super-8 showings at his studio at Butler's Wharf, pacing while rubbing his head with both hands, talking all the time while his public, made up of close friends, exchanged subtle eye rolling looks? Or because we didn't understand at the time that his child-like enthusiasm was in fact a quality. Or was it because a Nizo camera felt a bit amateurish? The beauty of his Super-8 movies was revealed to me when I saw them years later, properly projected on gallery walls, all at the same time. Stunning! Or was it because when he entered the Alternative Miss World competition, he put so much energy into it that it would have been cruel not to give him the crown. Derek was Derek and nobody really minded because his agitated energy was always positive.

Sebastiane (1976), the low budget movie 101, was his transition from artist to commercial artist. Since he loved people, it was easy for him to work with them. His work was his social life. He had been a student at the Slade School of Art with David Hockney, and Hockney's success must have been like an adrenaline shot for those he left behind, inspiring them to rise to the surface.

Derek's paintings of poles, rocks and figures [of the 1970s] against a plain background might seem reserved in comparison to the colourful palette of Hockney, but they could not be more British. More than paintings, I like to think that they are his early 'garden wish': imaginary gardens until he got in his garden at Prospect Cottage.

I am glad that my last meeting with Derek happened in his garden. There, for the first time, I realised he had finally created his masterpiece (I never had the courage to see his movie *Blue*, 1993). He created such a personal and magical place, perfectly at home in its bleak surroundings! Having spent the last 30 years of my life living with a gardener, I have visited many gardens, and none I have seen has ever surpassed the originality of Derek's. It is my favorite work of his, and it encompasses his paintings, set design, sculpture, gardening and love.

If my last memory of Derek is in his garden, my most favorite one is walking through the hobs-smelling Brick Lane of the East End of London to go and have breakfast: smoked haddock cooked in milk with a big slice of buttered bread.

Derek Jarman as Miss Crêpe Suzette, laureate of Alternative Miss World 1975

ACTION!
SIMON FISHER TURNER

Derek was and still is the imagining spirit of experimentation. Just shut your eyes and wonder what on earth he'd be making now with his mobile phone and social media recorders and probably no care for money whatsoever. The DJ channel on YouTube, musique concrète. Daily chat shows and interviews with all the most interesting people in the world. Sex films, gardening documentaries. He is and was the most colourful man I've ever met. I don't even have to shut my eyes to see him or hear him. He is still present whenever I need a chat or a little think. He is always on hand in my mind's eye.

We met by accident and somehow worked together over five feature films. I've no idea how this happened. I never asked for work, but was just in the right place at the right time. I was keen, and fast, but he was faster than us all. Over time a small group of us surrounded him and were the moons to his Starship. He was the boss, but an open man with a mind that was as curious as any child. His knowledge of the world we lived in was vast, and I learnt a great deal about life from this man, whether fact or fiction, art or music, drama or pretence. He was passionate. We found ourselves in extraordinary situations. We filmed each other, recorded conversations, made cakes together, walked and talked the shingles of Dungeness or the streets of Soho, or Edinburgh. We all worked with a passion and fun you can hardly believe.

I first made music for him as we shot *The Tempest* (1979) in Stoneleigh Abbey. Come the weekend, anyone not returning to London stayed on and we made happenings and recitals with Heathcote Williams and Jack Birkett. We were partying and creating constantly. I had a Revox reel-to-reel tape recorder and a keyboard and FX pedals. We all had a hand in the cooking and we let ourselves go once the cameras were off.

Derek had crazy ideas. One was for me to play a reporter interviewing Prospero on Concord on the way to New York. Prospero was to be played by Terry-Thomas, the ancient and rather grand English actor. It never came to be, but I travelled to Ibiza with a producer to try to entice him out of retirement to make this idea come true. Guy Ford and I took a case of wine as a gift. He was too old and fragile, sadly, but these kinds of ideas passed through Derek's mind every day. 'Let's make an Indian musical', he would say. Wouldn't it be brilliant.

I worked on *Sloane Square: A Room of One's Own* (1974–1976) which is all Super-8. The music was made in my girlfriend's flat with a four-track cassette recorded (borrowed) with a wasp synth, a radio and a bass guitar. We ran the film projected on the wall. Madness. I wish I had a picture. We were poor and that helped, I think. Less Is More.

I worked on *Caravaggio* (1986) getting the extras, then acting in it, and eventually Derek asked me to do the score. I had no idea how. You know, we were all learning at the same time how this all happened. Mistakes were made, and often Derek liked them. Now there's a good lesson. Embrace your mistakes.

I think I loved his experimental films better than anything because the images were so new and dangerous and colourful. I'd never seen anything like them in my life. Both *The Last of England* (1987) and *The Garden* (1990) have scenes of such beauty one can't even imagine how they were made. Thinking about it now of course, so much film was also left on the floor as it were, edited out. I was edited out of *Edward II* (1991). I spent a day in a suit of armour as Edward I. I made the book, the T-shirt, but not the final edit. Cut. Goodbye. What a time that was.

'Action'. I loved hanging out with Derek and Tilda on the coast. He would go off with her and the camera, and I'd head in the opposite direction recording sounds on the Ness. We never did nothing, but it didn't really seem like work, did it. We watched *Blind Date* on TV huddled under duvets. The power station might let off steam, or the lighthouse might warn the ships. Never silent on the Ness.

Simon Fisher Turner and Derek Jarman in *Blue*, 1993

The washing machine is whirring on its first wash of the day and I think of DJ for the first time today. The sun is out and a daffodil memory sweeps in with the rays and the distant roar of the sea as the tide is in. Shingle memories,

Blue (1993), *The Last of England*, *The Garden* all partially shot by the coast. Burning the stubble in the fields near Rye. Mr Punch and Judy never made it into the film visually, but sonically yes, they were in. Power station walks and into the hinterland behind the cottage and across the railway tracks. Hiding with Tilda. A perfect Hide and Seek location.

Edward II filming at Bray Studios. Rising at five to start the day. Derek missed some days, so Ken Butler took over. A wonderful atmosphere to film in. Chris Hobbs' vast sets reminding me of the *Caravaggio* shoot in East London Docklands. I must write my Jarman book. I must pass it on, or let the memories fade with the outgoing tide.

GBH, JUBILEE AND PUNK
JON SAVAGE

The footage is grainy and dark: black, white and grey, shakily shot in close focus. It shows four young men, all with short haircuts: a concentrating guitarist, an exhortatory bassist and a lead singer – in constant motion, at once grappling mid-song with an audience member before cavorting on stage. He is wearing pegged lurex-striped pants and a T-shirt that shows a naked footballer. Everything is sharp angles and quick motion. In its chiaroscuro and blurry texture, this brief clip could almost be a Slater Bradley recreation, imagining the visual record that should exist of an important cultural event.

But this does exist: the first ever footage taken of the Sex Pistols, by Derek Jarman at Andrew Logan's loft, on Valentine's Day 1976. Pictures of the event show a short-haired Jarman in the sparse crowd, holding a Super-8 camera as the world shifts. 'I didn't know who they were at that stage', Jarman told me[1]; 'There were about ten or 15 people there, and Jordan and Vivienne (Westwood) were in the front row egging them on and gobbing at them and pretending to have battles with them. I remember having to be careful with the camera even with that small number of people there, 'cos it was all over the place.'

The Sex Pistols' appearance was constructed by Malcolm McLaren to exploit a generation gap: the Andrew Logan crowd had been a major part of London's countercultural life since the early 1970s and by this stage were all in their early 30s. The Sex Pistols were all in their early 20s, if that, and were being promoted by McLaren as his instrument for creating a new pop generation of bored teenagers. Jarman later gave Jordan a lot of credit for not falling for this divisive rhetoric: 'She didn't make the differentiation between generations that the musicians or Malcolm or Vivienne did.'

It was Jordan who inspired Jarman's second feature film (*Jubilee*, 1978). The film-maker had been struck by her presence when he saw her in London's Victoria Station in 1974–1975: 'She was just a very startling image, more than anything I'd ever seen.

1 The quotes by Derek Jarman come from an interview I did with him in 1988 for *England's Dreaming*, Faber and Faber, London 1991. I met Derek in 1981, at a Brion Gysin show at the October Gallery in London. We became friends and spent a couple of summers driving through the Docklands east of London. An account of these voyages can be found in *Caught by the River: A Collection of Words on Water* (ed. Andrew Walsh, Jeff Barrett, and Robin Turner, Octopus, London 2009). I remained friends with him until his death. Since then, I have written for various publications about his work – including *Derek Jarman Super-8* (ed. Julia Stoschek, Walther König, Cologne 2010) and *Derek Jarman's Sketchbooks* (ed. Stephen Farthing and Ed Webb-Ingall, Thames & Hudson, London 2013). I was the co-curator, with Fiona Corridan, of the exhibition *Derek Jarman Protest!* at Manchester Art Gallery in 2021.

She was wearing white patent high heels and a very short miniskirt with a plastic, almost see-through front, and a T-shirt, and a beehive-ish hairstyle. Very blonde. I think it was Egyptian makeup at the time, and she looked stunning. I wasn't in any way aware of punk at that stage.'

After the success of the historical romp *Sebastiane* (1976), Jarman wanted to film something more contemporary: his wish to engage with the new aesthetic can be seen in the 1974–1976 Super-8 *Sloane Square: A Room of One's Own*, where he and a few friends are shown vandalising the Sloane Square apartment from which he had just been evicted. Like any artist with his or her antennae open to social shifts, Jarman could feel the chill blowing through British society, against which Punk was a reaction. As he told me, 'the genesis of *Jubilee* was originally a Super-8 film with Jordan, it wasn't anything to do with punk in that sense'.

'It was to do with Jordan and whatever she wanted to make, but it grew in the course of early 1977, while we were writing it, and it was Jordan who brought in the punk element, because we wanted musicians involved. Jordan specifically brought in Adam Ant, whom she was working with. Gradually one person introduced another. Siouxsie and the Banshees came along, and we did videos of all of these bands – the Slits, the Banshees, Adam, Chelsea and Wayne County. I knew Chelsea's Gene October already, 'cos he'd been around the gay clubs for years, and he felt he could fit in here.'

Jarman's genius was to recognise, although he was not of the same generation and could have dismissed the movement outright, that British Punk was an ambitious and deeply felt aesthetic that aimed to analyse, provoke and transform the state of the nation. Like the fanzines that flourished in the first few months of 1977, *Jubilee* is a highly collaged allegory that merges the two Queen Elizabeths: the 16th-century version (QEI) is seen in a series of hieratic, lush settings, while the 20th-century version (QEII) is brutally murdered in a derelict landscape.

Jubilee is saturated in Punk: not just with the musicians, but in the clothing and set design. The characters wear T-shirts and bondage trousers from Vivienne Westwood's Seditionaries or boiler suits emblazoned with painted slogans, like the early Clash, while Sex Pistols imagery – posters and news reports – is seen throughout. The whole cut-up feel and acceleration of Punk is counterposed with scenes of urban dereliction – mainly filmed in London's Docklands, which has its own description, postmodern, graffitied on a brick wall.

The narrative ends on a cautionary note. Despite the gang's extreme postures and casual, homicidal violence, they are taken up by a Rupert Murdoch-like media impresario Borgia Ginz – played, with tremendous, lip-smacking relish by Lindsay Kemp's former associate, Jack Birkett – who whisks them off to a Dorset mansion. The county is protected by barbed wire and customs officers – 'blacks, homosexuals and Jews are banned in Dorset' – not that that bothers the girl gang, now recast as Ginz's latest pop group, the Daughters of God, one whit.

Jordan's Dance, 1977

Jubilee was both accurate and ambivalent. A complex, contradictory film, it was hardly designed to appeal to the Punk audience that it simultaneously parodied and celebrated. On its release in February 1978, it got mixed reviews: sympathetic from the broadsheet newspapers, hostile and vindictive – to a man – from the music press. The unkindest cut came from an incandescent missive, printed on a T-shirt by Vivienne Westwood, that excoriated the film and Jarman himself in terms which would now be considered extremely homophobic.

The film's controversial reception helped to ensure Jarman's continuing career as a film-maker, as well as plugging him into a new generation of artists and film-makers such as Jordan, John Maybury, Kenny Morris of the Banshees. The film's foray into the cutting edge of pop culture also opened up the possibilities of the future collaborations with pop musicians that would be so important to him in the 1980s.

When Jarman's film career was put on hold for several years after *The Tempest* (1979), he found work directing pop films and videos for artists as diverse as Marianne Faithfull (*Broken English*, 1979), Throbbing Gristle (*TG Psychic Rally in Heaven*, 1981), Orange Juice (*What Presence?!*, 1984), Marc Almond (*Tenderness Is a Weakness*, 1984), Bryan Ferry (*Windswept*, 1985) and the Smiths (*Ask* and the short film *The Queen Is Dead*, both 1986). As well as providing much-needed income, these films kept Jarman current at the same time as they informed his film-making practice.

Always attuned to the nuances of power, Jarman took freely from Punk's desire to address the state of the nation. An insider/outsider, he was never bound by the confines of class and occupation: indeed, his life and work elided the boundaries between film, painting, montage, autobiography, the past and the present. He was highly ambivalent about England – at once celebrating its numinous countryside, while at the same time protesting the country's treatment of homosexuals, and berating the philistinism of the Thatcher government.

These complex feelings found expression in the *GBH* (for Grievous Bodily Harm) paintings of 1983–1984, huge black and red works that depicted the distinctive outline of England, Scotland and Wales consumed by fire and, in some cases, a funeral wreath. Jarman was using black backgrounds during this period – thickly applied in viscous oil paint, with no attempt to smooth its application – and this, combined with the dark red colour, expressed anger, hostility and indeed, in the combination, the black and red of anarchists.

This anger at the state of the country, together with Jarman's immersion in music and his expertise in collage, found its full expression in *The Last of England* (1987), a furious polemic against the state of what he perceived as a degraded and cruel nation, cut fast to music with the momentum he had learned from making pop videos. The accompanying book amplified the themes of the film and the *GBH* paintings: 'Fire informs *The Last of England*, burning, burning, burning. Can there be too much fire?'

The Punk wish to confront and expose taboos – plus its insistence on the instantaneity of art practice: do it fast, do it now – also inform Jarman's final series of paintings [the *Queer Paintings*, 1992–1993], which address his infection with AIDS and his certain death, rocket-fuelled by his anger at HIV sufferers' treatment at the hands of the media. Just as Punk critiqued the tabloids, so paintings like *Queer* and *Sex Horror* (both 1992) lay thick scrawls on top of multiple images of hostile and prejudiced front pages, saying what at the time was unsayable in simple and graphic terms.

In Jarman's long and complex life and career, Punk stands as a pivotal point between generations, between aesthetics, between pleasure and rumination and active engagement. Jarman was long fascinated by class, sexuality and power politics, which informed his collaged and inclusive aesthetic. Punk sharpened his anger and attack, and projected him forward into the polemical and critical artist that he became: one of the very few to make the struggle against the cruelties of 1980s Conservatism – the New Right – overt and effective.

NO KNOWN ADDRESS… OR DON'T LOOK DOWN… TILDA SWINTON

* A version of this text appeared in The Guardian on 17 August 2002, reproducing a speech given by Tilda Swinton at the Edinburgh Film Festival as part of a tribute to Derek Jarman. It has also been published in the catalogue *Derek Jarman: Brutal Beauty*, Serpentine Gallery/Koenig Books, London 2008, p. 10–17. It is reproduced in this volume with the kind permission of Tilda Swinton.

Dear Derek,

Jubilee is out on DVD. I found a copy in Inverness and watched it last night. It's as cheeky a bit of inspired old ham punk spunk nonsense as ever grew out of your brain and that's saying something: what a buzz it gives me to look at it now. And what a joke: there's nothing an eighth as mad bad and downright spiritualised being made down here these days this side of Beat Takashi. There's an interview with you at the end of the thing: a *Face to Face*... very nice to see that face, I must say. Jeremy Isaacs asks you, last of all, how you would like to be remembered and you say you would like to disappear. That you would like to take all your works with you and... evaporate...

It's a funny thing, because the truth is that here, eight years later, in so many ways you never could, but, it has to be faced, in so many others, you have. It's snowed since you were here and your tracks are covered. Fortunately you made them on hard ground.

Well, I could tell you that we got some things right, back then, sitting round the kitchen table in Dungeness, projectile vomiting with the best of them: you were INDEED the great Thatcherite film-maker – for every £200,000 film you made, real profits were seen – by someone or other – within at least the first two years, all those royal circus brides did indeed end up cutting themselves out of their wedding dresses and looking into the camera. Alan 'all-film-is-an-advertisement-for-something' Parker did end up running the BFI and dissolving its production arm, Film 4 WAS just a flash in the pan... I DID have twins of all genders and head for the hills.

Do you remember Norman Stone's call to arms about us all in the *Sunday Times*? Saying *The Last of England* and *Sammy and Rosie Get Laid* (Stephen Frears, 1987) and *Raining Stones* (Ken Loach, 1993) and I can't remember what else were a damaging and misleading series of slanders on the British character and profile?... those were the days. That strictly for export word 'British'... reminds me always how on show it encourages us to consider ourselves. Surely the idea of a national identity was always tricky enough: it strikes me any attempt to define a national identity for film is not unlike trying to get a hairnet on a jellyfish... and, by the by, not unreasonable to suggest that those in the definition business – boardroom table dancers with pension plans and jobs to lose – might not necessarily be best equipped to blue sky the blue for the rest of us.

They talk about The British Film Industry a lot these days. You remember that renaissance they all got moist about in the 1980s after *Chariots of Fire* (Hugh Hudson, 1981) won Oscars: the British are coming? And then that Kenneth Branagh thing with *Henry V* (1989)? Didn't he even call his company Renaissance Films? Well, the renaissances are rolling themselves out pretty much yearly, now, as director after director makes his or her first film and then graduates to making commercials.

The fact is – you know why – I cannot ever quite be serious about the British Film Industry. It's not a phrase I can use – could ever use – with much of a straight face. It's really nothing personal. It's just that I find I predate it, like I predate the thinking-man's stocks and shares, and I haven't quite got with the groove. Do you remember, we saw them setting up the stall in the empty field, and the tiny man with the megaphone settling himself into position behind the imperial velvet curtain? We were there watching when the wily colonial entrepreneur circled the ring at the village fête with hot hands, and did visible dollar sums in his head at the sight of the handicraft table, and prepared to hand over bead necklaces to the cottage weavers for their finger-woven items from hand-reared indigenous materials – it felt like industrial films on these islands in those 1980s were made by people who could not quite get into television. Or by shameless traitorous ex-patriots who had legged it for the free world in the colonies. In those days, British Film, when invoked, meant getting proud about *The Lavender Hill Mob* (Charles Crichton, 1951) or *Whisky Galore*

Derek Jarman and Tilda Swinton, Berlin, c. 1986

(Alexander Mackendrick, 1949). An American/Indian partnership began to give Britain an exportable identity: these were the Crabtree and Evelyn Waugh days of ex-imperial mooning about, when nostalgic dreams of The Grand Tour meant film culture to a lot of people. Class obsession, still, now, the greatest stock in the trade of industrial cinema here, began to show a profit. 'Gotcha' became a word in the national anthem. Land of banal hope, of Past Times glory... still superior about the land of the free on the grounds that we managed to sell London Bridge to the desert... who's the colony, though? Then and now...

I had run away to join a different circus, myself – yours: Planet Jarmania – you were the first person I met who could gossip about Saint Thomas Aquinas and hold a steady camera at the same time as you did at our first meeting... I thought it would be good to hang out with you for six weeks... I guess we had things to say. Our outfit was an internationalist brigade. Decidedly pre-industrial, a little loud, a tot louche. Not always in the best possible taste. And not quite fit, though it saddened and maddened us to recognise it, for wholesome family entertainment.

Wholesome families were all the rage then. There was a fashion for a thing called 'normal' and there was a plague abroad called 'perversion'. There was no such thing as society, and culture meant something to do with a yoghurt plant. This was before the *Sunday Times* educated us that culture means digested opinions about marketable artistic endeavours. Things are a little different now: people – at least pretend to – have an enormous amount of sex and tell everybody else about it. Not much *Butterflies* on telly, except on the nostalgia channels. We use the word 'terrestrial' without a flicker of spacethink. People cook and decorate their flats and celebrate the millennium and the opening of the Commonwealth Games in Manchester after compatible Cajun/Echo Park hacienda/Alternative Miss World c. 1978 styles. Straight has started to mean honest again, getting very drunk is hilariously funny and smart, and newsreaders would refer to today as July 17th.

And there's a big chat on about film culture now that means... genuinely concerned and frustrated individuals scrupulously trying to drum up and contextualise a cinema that speaks to them... I tend to have a kind of visual/aural dysphasia with that phrase and end up thinking that what is being championed is a sort of film couture, as distinct from the ready-to-wear or diffusion line cinema that it's always easier to find off the peg... I suppose there's some kind of balance to that analogy: although the fashion world – the business that fashion is – is at least cynical enough to understand the loss-leading value of the mystique of the handstitched and the Marie Antoinette fantasy about seamstresses losing their eyesight in exchange for their passionate toil over the bugle beads. That old garret mythology... it doesn't half send shivers of glee down the spines of the Uber-rich – it's a fantasy not only of patronage but also some sort of sacrificial blood drinking... the secret, if not of eternal youth, then of eternal spiritual worth... an artist suffered for me...

We used to be referred to as 'arthouse'; how it used to irk us then... how disparaging it sounded... how sickly and highfalutin', pious and extracurricular. For 'arthouse superstar' read 'jumbo shrimp'. Yet, then, as now, the myth prevailed that there was only ever one mainstream. We were only too happy to know that our audience existed and to hoe the row in peace. Nobody here paid that much attention to us, that's true: no one ever thought we might make them any money, I suppose. What grace that constituted. Not to be identified as national product... The intergalactic BFI. ZDF in Germany. Mikado in Italy. Uplink in Japan. This was our nation state: this was continuity. We snuck under the fence, looked for – and found – our fellow travellers elsewhere. Here's a thought: slice the world longways, along its lines of sensibility, and not straight up and down, through its geographical markers, and company will be yours, young film-maker Company, continuity, identity. Treason? To what?

The dead hand of Good Taste has commenced its last great attempt to buy up every soul on the planet, and from where I'm sitting, it's going great guns.

Art is now indivisible from the idea of culture: culture from heritage: heritage from tourism: tourism from what I saw emblazoned recently on the window of an American chainstore in Glasgow as 'the art of leisure'. That means, incidentally, velour lounge suits by the ton.

The colonial balance has shifted and the long spoons are out. We now stand shoulder to shoulder with something as identifiable as Civilisation itself, or else... Security never felt so much like a term of abuse. I was in Los Angeles earlier this year and was asked by a jeweller's assistant – in a hypergrand jewellery emporium on Rodeo Drive – if the reason I declined to wear a stars and stripes jewelled badge on my front at a public event was because I was, in fact, an 'Afghani bitch'...

You may not need me to tell you about the fight for civilisation afoot these days. More of the same but worse than even you could have imagined. Meanwhile, in a binary world, we on these islands cream on creamily up a Third Way. Things have got awfully tidy recently. There is a lot of finish on things. Clingfilm gloss and the neatest of hospital corners. The formula merchants are out in force. They are in the market for guaranteed product. Financial returns... add-water-and-stir reputations after one appearance over the parapet... the elusive second film – the developing body of work – far down that yellow brick road...

They go out looking for film-makers with the nous of one who might consider employing halogen spotlights in the hopes of attracting wild cats into a suburban garden. They are missing the point. Don't they know the roulette wheel is fixed? The croupier is a cardsharp? Do these people not watch old movies? It's the spirited that hold hands in the long run, it always was, the low key for the long term, the irreverent, the cheats, the undaunted and inspired rulebreakers, not the goody-goody industrial types with their bedside manners and managerial knowhow.

It is all done with smoke and mirrors and it always will be. Not with memos and corporate steering groups. Not with statistical evidence on test-screening audience feedback. Don't they know the basic laws of being in an audience? That we say we want to know more about the villain, but we don't really: that we say we like happy endings, but our souls droop without the bittersweet touch of something we might recognise – as we bend in from our fascinating and complex mortal world, into the virtual dark and back again. That we say we want famous faces we can recognise, but there's a thing – a face – that we identify as an actor's – first and foremost – cannot do for us that the face we might see as that of a person can do. It's human beings that are of use to use in the figurative cinema. Human shapes and gauchenesses and human passions, not drama and perfect timing and a well-tuned charisma round every bend.

I have always wholeheartedly treasured in your work the whiff of the school play. It tickles me still and I miss it terribly. I forage for it now in the films I make with Lynn Hershman.[1] The antidote it offers to the mirrorball of the marketable – the artful without the art, the meaningful devoid of meaning is meat and drink to so many of us looking for that dodgy wig, that moment of awkward zing, that loose corner: where we might prise up the carpet and uncover the rich slates of something we might recognise as spirit underneath. Something raw and dusty and inarticulate, for heaven's sake. This is what Pasolini knew. What Rosselini knew. What Abbas Kiarostami knows. This is also what Ken Loach knows. What Andrew Kotting knows. What Bill Douglas knew. What Michael Powell and Emeric Pressburger, what William Blake, knew. And, for that matter, what Caravaggio knew, painting prostitutes as Madonnas and rent boys as saints; no – Madonnas as prostitutes and saints as rent boys... there's the rub. It's all about rhythm: it's all in the knees. Bring it from home. Bring it out from under your bed. Your own bed. Your own life. That's – eventually – what you did, Derek, and measures your highest contribution as an artist, in my opinion: that you made your work out of the soup kitchen that was your life.

I think that the reason that people wanted to inaugurate this event in your name, the reason that you count for so much, so uniquely, to some people, particularly in this hidebound little place we call home, is that you lived so clearly the life that an artist lives. Your money was where your mouth was always. Your vocation – and here maybe it helped a little that you offered that special combination of utter self-obsession with the appearance of the kindest Jesuit classics master in the school – was a spiritual one, even more than it was political, even more than it was artistic. And the clarity with which you offered up your life and the living of it, particularly since the epiphany – I can call it nothing less – of your illness, was a genius stroke, not only of provocation, but of grace. Your gesture of public confessional, both within and without your

1 Lynn Hershman Leeson (b. 1941) is an American visual artist and director who, with Tilda Swinton in the female lead, directed *Conceiving Ada* (1997) and *Teknolust* (2002).

work – at a time when people talked fairly openly about setting up ostracised HIV island communities and others feared, not only for their lives, but, believe it or not, also for their jobs, their insurance policies, their friendships, their civil rights – was made with such particular and characteristically inclusive generosity that it was at that point that you made an impact far outspanning the influence of your work... you made your spirit, your nature, known to us – and the possibility of an artist's fearlessness a reality. And the truth is: by defying it, you may have changed the market as well...

There is a character in Fellini's *La Dolce Vita* (1960) – shall I leave out that he is the suicide? – who describes himself: 'too serious to be a dilettante, too much of a dabbler to be a professional'. I use it in my own head from time to time to explain to myself, if to no one else, my peculiar idle ways. Now I look at it again, I think of you and how it might well describe you. Your focus on the ball beyond the crowd. Your amateur's enthusiasm. Your delight in process. Your perennial beginner's mind.

Things you taught me: Huckleberry Finn getting a fence painted by having such a visibly good time doing one post himself that every passer-by stops to join in. And never to leave a place having done all you want to do there.

You should have been a Catholic, I sometimes think, Del. All those robes in *Caravaggio*, all those poppies in *War Requiem* and again in *The Last of England* and *The Garden*, to say nothing of all that buggery in the crypt in *Jubilee*... you and Michael Powell have to be the best subscribers to the passionate use of cardinal red in English cinema. The secret language of holy blood in the hands of the pagans... long live the passion. Why is it that the English never mention that Shakespeare was a Catholic? All those squeaky scrubbed classical columns. The colour-free reformation. Clean up the sweat and blood, if not the tears. Here we go again. Long live sweat. Long live secret blood. There's more than one way to organise a clearance.

A lot of people go to Dungeness nowadays. I expect you know that from Keith. Those old stones: you said they'd grow things and they did. When I think of that nice lady who showed us round Prospect Cottage that day we found it. How quiet, how pale pink her bedroom was there. I wonder where she went. Do you remember that letter we found under the carpet with the old rubber johnny in it: '... my wife is not a cold woman but... you are so lovely... ' some such. Addressed to a woman in Vauxhall, as I remember. And never sent. Under the carpet with it before she comes in... aah. Unsent letters.

I found this again the other day: this is Emeric Pressburger writing to the actress Wendy Hiller outlining the Archers MO [his film production company with Powell] in the hopes of persuading her to work with them on *The Life and Death of Colonel Blimp* (1943):

One: we owe allegiance to nobody except the financial interests which provide our money and to them the sole responsibility of ensuring them a profit not a loss.

Two: every single foot in our films is our own responsibility and nobody else's. we refuse to be guided or coerced by any influence but our own judgement.

Three: when we start work on a new idea we must be a year ahead, not only of our competitors, but also of the times. a real film, from idea to universal release, takes a year. or more.

Four: no artist believes in escapism. and we secretly believe that no audience does. we have proved, at any rate, that they will pay to see the truth, for other reasons than her nakedness.

Five: at any time, and particularly at the present, the self-respect of all collaborators, from star to prop-man, is sustained, or diminished, by the theme and purpose of the film they are working on. they will fight or intrigue to work on a subject they feel is urgent or contemporary, and fight equally hard to avoid working on a trivial or pointless subject. and we agree with them and want the best workmen with us; and get them. these are the main things we believe in. they have brought us an unbroken record of success and a unique position. without the one of course we should not have enjoyed the other very long. we are under no illusions. we know we are surrounded by hungry sharks. but you have no idea what fun it is surf-bathing, if you have only paddled, with a nurse holding onto your rompers. we hope you will come on in, the water's fine.

Here's a tradition speaking: and it's a tradition that you belong to, Derek: and those of us whose hearts rise up to the challenge fall in alongside the best company possible on these islands... a long-established – and classical, some might argue – national tradition of powerful outsider artists... pioneers... devoted to the idea of making things not made before... shapes and gestures new to the lexicon... people willing to trust the law that humanity and human-made work is good for humanity... at least that it's better for them to make than not to make... that society's shapes and patterns, at heart, cannot be as profoundly fascinating as the humans that live within them, and that they are not alone.

That earlier *Jubilee* year you gave us prophecy: painting extinct in Paranoia Paradise, the generation who grew up and forgot to lead their lives, the idea of artists as the world's blood donors, history written on a Mandrax, fear of dandelions... and yet, like Carnation from Floris, not all the good things have disappeared.

Maybe it's as bad as you and I used to say it could possibly get, now. Maybe it's worse. But here we are, the rest of us, tilting at the sameold sameold windmills and spooking at the same old ghosts. And keeping company, all the same. It's a rotten mess of a shambles, you could say. It's driving into the curve, at the very least. Some would say you are well out of it. I reckon you would say let me at 'em.

I say bring it on. Bring on the fisticuffs and let's get weaving. And that we could do with you here among us. And I can't be the only one, 'cos look: hey, you're a memorial lecture now and look: hey, stranger still, I'm giving it. Are they tired of the academic view, one wonders, tired of the need to listen to lectures about funding bodies and cultural diversity? What do they want to hear about from me? What can I give them?

Given that it's you who should be the one standing here giving your own memorial lecture – not for the first time, your closest friends might cry – and you are presently otherwise engaged, or at least have left the building, I suppose I might as well read them this and let them in on the trick – that the conversation is not done yet... that the company you keep with us, when we care to think of it, is just as strong and empowering as it ever was. That the example you set is as simple as a logo to sell a sports shoe; less chat, more action, less fiscal reports, more films, less paralysis, more process. Less deference. More dignity. Less money. More work. Less rules. More examples. Less dependence. More love.

It has nothing whatever to do with money. Money is the easiest thing in the world for any film-maker to come by: next to vision, stamina, vocation, resourcefulness, comradeship, a sense of the ridiculous, and the long, long view, money grows on trees. Money is the one element that socialises a film-maker – that... ties him to the shore. Easier to control, easier to scupper... who's for Emeric's surf-bathing?

A suggestion about money: keep it clean. Have less. Need less. Want less. Work with straw, but work.

And the challenges facing a film culture here?

> The possibility of film-makers losing the use of their own spirits.
> The paralysis of isolated original voices.
> The existence of the student loan in place of the student grant.
> The rarity of distributers with kamikaze vision.
> The habit of patronage.
> Too many conference tables.
> Too few cinemas.
> Too little patience.
> Pomp and circumstance.
> The concept of the 'successful' product.
> The idea that there is not enough to go around.
> The eye to the main chance.
> The substitution of co-dependence for independence.
> The idea that it has to cost millions of pounds to make a feature film.
> The idea that there is only one way to skin a cat.

W.H. Auden to B. Britten: 'Goodness and beauty result from a combination of order and chaos, bohemianism and bourgeois convention... bohemianism alone leads to a mad jumble of beautiful scraps... bourgeois convention alone to large unfeeling corpses.'

This is what I miss, there being no more Derek Jarman films: the mess the vulgarity the cant the poetry the edge the pictures Simon Fisher Turner's music the real faces the intellectualism the science the bad temperedness the good temperedness the cheek the standards the anarchy the gaucheness the romanticism the classicism the optimism the activism the challenge the longeurs the glee the playfulness the bumptiousness the resistance the wit the fight the colours the grace the passion the goodness the beauty.

Long livemess. Longlivepassion. Longlivecompany.

Yr, Tild
Easter Ross, Scotland, September 2002

WAR PAINT
SIMON WATNEY

1 Gay Left: http://gayleft1970s.org/ (last accessed September 2024).

I first met Derek Jarman in the mid-1970s. I had recently completed an MA at The Courtauld Institute and was supporting myself through part-time teaching. Actively involved in the arena of queer politics and culture, I was living in a squat in Stoke Newington together with five other people. Of the three gay men who lived there, I am now the only survivor. Haoui Montaug (1952–1991) went on to become an illustrious figure in the queer counter-culture of New York in the 1980s, while the Australian documentary film-maker Philip Brooks (1953–2003) became one of the founders of the annual Paris lesbian and gay film festival, together with his partner Laurent Bocahut. Having moved to London from Brighton in 1974, I had been a volunteer at the Lesbian and Gay Switchboard since 1985, and two years later I joined The Gay Left Collective.[1] I had been closely involved in national queer politics ever since the foundation of the Gay Liberation Front movement, but my contacts with the creative avant-garde of the mid-1970s were mainly through dance and movement classes, as well as my friendships with film-maker Ron Peck (1948–2022) and art critic Stuart Morgan (1948–2002).

Unlike Derek, I was very much into the mainstream gay nightclub dance scene. All my life I had been passionate about American R&B and soul music, and I was far more interested in the latest Italian clothes arriving in the boutiques of Soho than in the zips and safety-pins of punk *couture*. In this respect, I could not have been less like Derek. Alongside my queer political instincts, I had been very involved in supporting the campaign to join the European Common Market (EU as is) as a committed Eurocommunist, inspired by the political vision of Enrico Berlinguer (1922–1984).

What Derek and I initially shared was a strong attraction to the world of museums and galleries, and in particular to the world of Elizabethan and Stuart England, from its architecture and decorative arts to its poetry, stagecraft and pageantry. In my case this involved a particular passion for sculptural church monuments, and Derek and I enjoyed visiting churches together. Indeed, he was the only person I knew who was as familiar with London's City churches as with the churches of Florence and Rome, and I have a list somewhere of the places in Rome which he thought it was necessary to visit, setting out from the Hotel Croce di Malta on the Via del Babuino near the Spanish Steps.

I was seven years younger than Derek, which means more in one's 20s and 30s than in later life. We had several friends and acquaintances in common, including the artist Robert Medley (1905–1994) who I knew via our mutual longstanding friendship with Duncan Grant (1885–1978). It was thus inevitable that, like several of my friends from the world of Lesbian and Gay Switchboard, I would be drawn into the wide circle of people who were regular visitors to Derek's studio at Butler's Wharf overlooking the River Thames, where in those years he held 'open house' on Saturday afternoons. He certainly struck me as very much a product of his generation of gay men, whose sense of identity was formed long before the emergence of Gay Liberation. This was apparent from his dedicated devotion to the idea of belonging to a timeless queer genealogy stretching back across time and space. It was an attitude he shared with other older gay men of my acquaintance. With me he could be confident that he could share references to the writings of Sir Thomas Browne (1605–1682) for example, or the sermons and poetry of John Donne (1572–1631), as well as his monument, which survived the Great Fire of London and is still to be found in St Paul's Cathedral. We also shared a deeply gratifying knowledge of the surviving houses of so many of the leading figures of the Elizabethan and Stuart Court. That was a rare pleasure for us both, given our shared commitment to the struggles of the contemporary world, in which not many people shared our historical interests. We knew few people like ourselves who were equally familiar with the theologically-charged triangular design of Borromini's church of Sant'Ivo alla Sapienza in Rome, and the remarkable triangular lodge built by the Catholic Sir Thomas Tresham in the 1590s in the heart of rural Northamptonshire.

This was the context of shared interests that informed our discussions of his latest film projects, beginning with *The Tempest* (1979). Over the years we talked, sometimes at length, at the early script-development stages of most of his feature films, and he also usually invited me in to see the final edit. I think he enjoyed trying ideas out with me not because he had any particular faith in my judgement, but because he knew that I was consistent in my views, and able and prepared to disagree with him if the need arose, as it often did. Being outside the repertory company he had assembled around himself over the years, he knew that my opinions were independent and disinterested. For example, I thought that *Caravaggio* (1986) was not helped by the lengthy monologues about the nature of art, realism and so on, in which I think his personal identification with Caravaggio got the better of him. Nor did I like or understand the figure of Judas Iscariot in *The Garden* (1990), and what I took to be the over-long, overly didactic scene concerning credit cards. From the outset however, I had no input whatsoever into his 1993 *Wittgenstein* film, his motivation for which entirely escaped me, and concerning which there was nothing I could usefully say. Nor did I have anything to contribute to his film of Benjamin Britten's *War Requiem* (1989).

Derek Jarman's studio during the making of the *Queer Paintings*, 1992

My involvement with Derek's work as a painter was quite distinct from my relationship, such as it was, to his film-making practice. We certainly talked a lot about Caravaggio in the early stages of the film project, which was sadly bent out of shape by the seemingly endless, time-consuming, distracting delays in funding. Few major artists have enjoyed a greater expansion of popular estimation in my lifetime than Caravaggio, whose career I had studied as an undergraduate art historian in the 1960s with the benefit of classes at the University of Sussex with Benedict Nicolson, the great Georges de la Tour scholar. Derek and I used to go to art exhibitions together, which was a great pleasure because he delighted in sharing his views and opinions with anyone who happened to be in the vicinity, as I have described elsewhere.[2]

On a more immediately practical level, Derek was always on the look-out for objects and images to use in his various collages, and when

2 Simon Watney, 'Derek Jarman, 1942–1994: A Political Death', *Artforum*, New York, vol. 32, issue 9, May 1994: www.artforum.com/features/derek-jarman-1942-1994-a-political-death-203058/ (last accessed September 2024).

he was in London at weekends he would usually be up early on Saturday mornings to get to the Stables Market in Camden Town, which in those days was a properly functioning collectors' market, and only a few streets away from where I lived throughout the 1980s and 1990s. I can remember him stopping off at my place one Saturday morning pushing an old wooden wheelbarrow full of bits and pieces he aimed to revitalise. Knowing his tastes, I also used to buy old gay erotica for him from the *Gay Treasures* store on Hudson Street in New York whenever I was there,[3] and several photographs I gave him eventually resurfaced in his work.

As the impact of HIV was gradually more deeply felt in the course of the 1980s, I became increasingly closely involved in the community-based educational response. I also wrote widely about the epidemic, including a book that focused on the highly distorted press coverage of the epidemic in Britain, which was one extreme expression of the growing bigotry of the Thatcher era. I had been an activist since my teenage years, and I was also one of the three co-founders of the OutRage! group in 1990 in response to growing anti-gay violence and homophobic legislation such as Section 28. This renewed current of activism in my life also served to deepen my friendship with Derek, who read my art criticism in places such as *Artforum*, as well as my writings in popular publications produced for the gay scene for which I had written since long before the epidemic. I quickly became a prolific writer about HIV/AIDS issues both in Britain and overseas. In the early years of the epidemic I was still teaching photographic studies at the School of Communication at the former Polytechnic of Central London (now the University of Westminster), where in 1985 I taught a course on the representation of HIV/AIDS that led to my book *Policing Desire: Pornography, AIDS & the Media*.[4]

One central aspect of my research for *Policing Desire* involved consideration of the British tabloid press, and I accumulated an extensive archive of front pages and other materials. I used these to make 35mm slides that formed the basis of talks and other public presentations that I gave at conferences and elsewhere. Derek was very drawn to this material, and in the late 1980s and early 1990s he used to visit my apartment periodically, and we would look through mountains of

3 Simon Watney, 'On Saturday Afternoons in 1963', *Photography & Culture*, vol. 4, issue 1, March 2011, p. 73–76.
4 Simon Watney, *Policing Desire: Pornography AIDS & The Media*, Cassell/ The University of Minnesota Press, London/Minneapolis 1997.

old newspaper clippings from my rapidly expanding collection. There was a commercial photocopying shop at the end of my street, and he would carry off large numbers of newspaper pages to be scanned, returning the originals to me and taking the large scanned sheets home with him to Soho. All the originals are now kept, together with the rest of my extensive HIV/AIDS related archives, in the library of the London School of Economics. Derek would have his photocopies duplicated and attached directly onto canvas, echoing Andy Warhol's working process.[5] Front-pages from *The Sun* that he selected include: 'Vile Book in School. Pupils See Pictures of Gay Lovers' (Tuesday, 6 May 1986); '18 Vice Boys in AIDS Revenge' (Monday, 24 November 1986); 'Gay Santa Gets Sack' (Saturday, 6 December 1986) and so on and so forth.

The underlying photocopied imagery is sometimes visible behind the heavily worked paint surfaces he applied. He would respond to this imagery with his own words, which he inscribed through the paint using a variety of different types of *sgraffiti*, as a type of amplification, adjusting his voice from a whisper to a scream. He employed this strategy in the production of most of his larger, late graffiti paintings, but also in his 1989 installation at the Third Eye Centre in Glasgow (now the CCA, see p. 6–7), where the walls were papered with photocopied tabloid front-pages, on which were mounted several tarred-and-feathered mattresses, surrounding a central, barbed-wire cage. This imprisoned two recumbent gay men on a mattress, and, briefly, his great friend and muse Tilda Swinton, prefiguring her solo performance at the Serpentine Gallery in London in *The Maybe* in 1995.[6] The raging anger that informs these late works stands in marked contrast to the impeccably polite persona that he unfailingly presented to the world.

I occasionally helped Derek with bits of research, especially as his eyesight failed, and I frequently read to him. In the last year of his life he very kindly undertook the screened décor for a fundraising concert by Suede that I had helped organise, but that is another story.[7]

Images from the documentary *Hating Peter Tatchell* by Christopher Amos, 2021

5 As far as I am aware, Derek Jarman never painting directly onto the pages of actual newspapers glued to canvas, as has been claimed, for instance in Norman Rosenthal, '"I have walked behind the sky": The Painter Who Became a Film-maker', in Seán Kissane and Karim Rehmani-White (eds.), *Derek Jarman Protest!*, Irish Museum of Modern Art/Thames & Hudson, Dublin/London 2020, p. 79–84.

6 See https://www.serpentinegalleries.org/whats-on/maybe/ (last accessed September 2024).

7 Suede concert at the Clapham Grand, 12 July 1993. See www.concertarchives.org/concerts/suede-siouxsie (last accessed September 2024).

Derek Jarman during a march organised by OutRage!, London, 6 February 1992

The G
HOM
GAYABANDON
REAL LIVES

CHRONOLOGY

Chronology compiled and expanded by Laetitia Chauvin based on Roger Wollen's chronology in *Derek Jarman: A Portrait*, Thames & Hudson, London 1996, reprinted in Seán Kissane and Karim Rehmani-White (eds.), *Derek Jarman Protest!*, Irish Museum of Modern Art/Thames & Hudson, Dublin/London 2020, p. 308–311. For a complete list of Jarman's Super-8 filmography and clips, see James Mackay's list and the chronology in ibid., p. 298–299 and p. 306.

Derek Jarman in front of *After Poussin's Inspiration of a Poet*, Priory Road Studio, 1966–1967

1942
– Born 31 January in Northwood, in south London. His father, Lancelot Elworthy Jarman, was born in New Zealand, and was an officer in the Royal Air Force. His mother, Elizabeth Evelyn Puttock, was born in India, and worked for a time for British fashion designer Norman Hartnell.

1942–1950
– Following military postings, the Jarman family lives in England, Pakistan and Italy.

1946–1960
– Jarman shows an aptitude and curiosity for gardening, drawing, literature, acting and stage design throughout his schooling.

The Jarman family at Dancing Ledge, 1956

1960
– Although he is accepted at the Slade School of Fine Art in London, Jarman decides to study literature, history and art history at King's College London to comply with his father's wishes. He nevertheless manages to attend drawing classes at the Slade and is introduced to the poetry of the Beat Generation.
– First exhibition at True Lovers' Knot in Northwood under the name Michael Derek Jarman.

1962
– First trips to France, Greece and Switzerland.

1963
– Moves to central London and starts to study painting at the Slade, specialising in scenography.

1964
– First visit to the United States.

1967
– Participation in the inaugural exhibition of the Lisson Gallery, founded by Nicholas Logsdail, a fellow student at the Slade who Jarman had encouraged to set up his own gallery. Jarman exhibits there in 1969 and 1970.
– Graduation followed by numerous exhibitions including *Young Contemporaries*, Tate Gallery, London; Edinburgh Open Hundred, Edinburgh; Ve Biennale des Jeunes Artistes, Musée d'Art Moderne de la Ville de Paris, Paris.
– First paintings of 'deserts' that combined mountain profiles and megaliths.

Derek Jarman, David Hockney and Ossie Clark at Jarman's birthday party, Sloane Square, London, 1968

Derek Jarman, Lisson Gallery, London, 1969

1967–1968
– Set and costume design for *Jazz Calendar*, choreography by Frederick Ashton and music by Richard Rodney Bennett for the Royal Ballet, Covent Garden, London. Collaboration on the scenography for John Gielgud's production of Mozart's *Don Giovanni* for the English National Opera.

Sketch for the set of *Jazz Calendar*, 1967

Rehearsal for *Jazz Calendar*, 1968, Royal Opera House, Covent Garden, London

1970
– Moves to Bankside Studio.
– Meets Ken Russell, who invites Jarman to design the sets for his film *The Devils*, based on Aldous Huxley's novel *The Devils of Loudun* (1952).
– Beginning of the production of *Studio Bankside*, his first Super-8 film, followed by a dozen others. Numerous scripts are also considered, but never shot.

Derek Jarman on the set of *The Devils* (1970) by Ken Russel, Pinewood Studios

1972
– Publication of his first book of poetry, *A Finger in the Fishes Mouth*.
– Creation of the sets for Russell's *Wild Messiah*, inspired by the life of the French sculptor Henri Gaudier-Brzeska (1891–1915).

1973
– Moves to 36 Butler's Wharf, where he lives until 1979.
– Designs a garden for the restaurant acquired by his sister, Gaye.
– Designs costumes for the ballet *Silver Apples of the Moon*, choreography by Tim Spain and music by Morton Subotnick.

1975
– Jarman, as Miss Crêpe Suzette, wins first prize in the third Alternative Miss World Competition organised by Andrew Logan.

1976
– Release of his first feature film, *Sebastiane*, shot in Sardinia, and entirely in Latin.
– First collaboration with the Sex Pistols on a video clip. Other collaborations follow, including with Marianne Faithfull, Throbbing Gristle, Orange Juice, the Pet Shop Boys, The Smiths and Bryan Ferry.

1978
– Release of the feature film *Jubilee*, starring Adam Ant, Jordan and Toyah Wilcox, chronicling life at the end of the 20th century, with references to Queen Elizabeth I (1533–1603), the alchemist John Dee (1527–1608) and the character of Ariel in William Shakespeare's *The Tempest* (1623).

1979
– Release of the feature film *The Tempest*, based on Shakespeare's play.
– Jarman moves to Charing Cross Road, his last London address, and begins to build his extensive library.

1982

– Designs sets and costumes for Igor Stravinsky's opera *The Rake's Progress* (1948–1951), directed by Ken Russell for the Teatro Maggio Musicale Firenze and set in contemporary England. First use of gold leaf for sets, soon also used in his paintings.

Set by Derek Jarman for an act of *The Rake's Progress* staged by Ken Russell, Florence, 1982

1984

– Publication of the first volume of his autobiographical writings, *Dancing Ledge*.

– Retrospective exhibition at the Institute of Contemporary Arts in London, bringing together more than 30 paintings, including the series of six large-format *GBH Paintings*, a critique of the repression and conservatism of Margaret Thatcher's government.

– Production of the short films *Imagining October*, shot in the USSR, and *The Angelic Conversation*, based on Shakespeare's sonnets.

Michael Clark dancing in Jarman's exhibition at the Institute of Contemporary Arts, London, 1982

1986

– After years of fund-raising and rewriting of the script, the feature film *Caravaggio* is released.

– Shortlisted for the Turner Prize for 'the visual quality of his films'. In the exhibition accompanying the prize, Jarman shows nine paintings in black paint and tar, a technique he has recently begun using, in which objects related to the film *Caravaggio* are integrated.

– Makes video clips for The Smiths.

– Jarman tests positive for HIV/AIDS on 22 December.

1987

– Release of the feature film *The Last of England*.

– Thanks to an inheritance from his father, he buys Prospect Cottage, Dungeness, Kent.

– Begins to assemble objects, usually found on the beach, and continues to produce tar paintings in which the combined elements are increasingly explicit (condoms, broken mirrors, rosaries, Hulk figurines).

– Jarman makes his HIV-positive status public and takes part in demonstrations, showing his disagreement with the policies of the Conservative British government.

– First exhibition at Richard Salmon Ltd, London, his gallery until 1994.

1989

– Artistic director for the Pet Shop Boys' tour of Hong Kong and Great Britain.

– Release of the feature film *War Requiem*.

– Exhibition of paintings at the Accattone cinema, Paris.

– Exhibition at the Third Eye Centre, Glasgow.

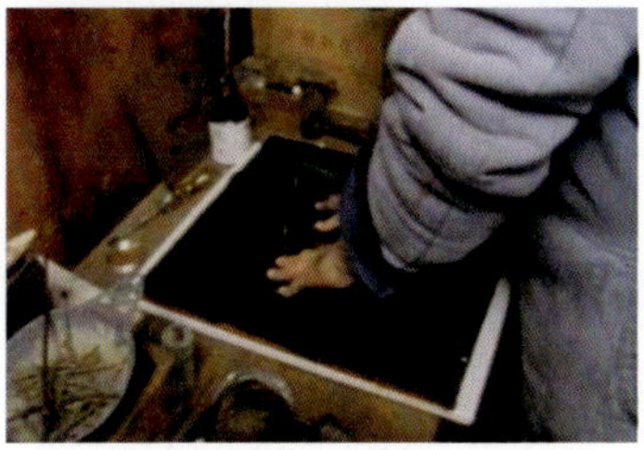

Image from the documentary *Derek Jarman. A Portrait* (1990) filmed by Mark Kidel

1990

– Release of the feature film *The Garden*.

1991

– Release of the feature film *Edward II*.

– Publication of his autobiographical diary *Modern Nature*.

– Under the name Saint Derek of Dungeness of the Order of Celluloid Knights, Jarman is canonised by the Sisters of Perpetual Indulgence, a non-conformist order created in 1979 whose vow is 'to expiate systematic guilt and promote universal joy'.

1992

– Publication of *At Your Own Risk. A Saint's Testament* about his fight against HIV/AIDS and his relationship with the media.

– The paintings depicting homophobic tabloid headlines in the *Queer Paintings* series are shown in his solo exhibition at the Manchester City Art Gallery, travelling in 1993 to the Palazzo delle Esposizioni in Rome and the Filmmuseum in Potsdam. His *Black Paintings* are filled with objects associated with illness and treatment: syringes, thermometers, drugs.

1993

– Release of the feature film *Wittgenstein*.

– First screening of the film *Blue* at the Venice Biennale.

1994

– Publication of *Chroma: A Book of Colour June '93*.

– Exhibition *Evil Queen, Last Paintings*, Whitworth Art Gallery, Manchester.

– Jarman dies on 19 February.

1995

– Posthumous publication of *Derek Jarman's Garden* with photographs by Howard Sooley.

1996

– Retrospective *Derek Jarman: Artist, Filmmaker, Designer*, Barbican Centre, London.

2008

– *Brutal Beauty* exhibition curated by Isaac Julien, Serpentine Gallery, London.

– First Film London Jarman Award given to Luke Fowler: annual prize of £10,000 awarded to artists in the field of the moving image, touring major cultural venues in England, Scotland, Wales and Northern Ireland.

– Publication of *Derek Jarman/Jean Cocteau. Alchimie* (Magic Cinéma, Bobigny 2008) to coincide with the exhibition of the same name organised as part of the 19th Festival Théâtres au cinéma in Bobigny. The book looks back at the links between the two creators and includes a full critical presentation of Jarman's filmography.

– The Luma Foundation acquires the original Super-8 films and takes charge of their restoration, conservation and distribution.

2013

– Amanda Wilkinson organises the first exhibition of works by Jarman. She officially represents the artist from 2017.

2018

– Death of Keith Collins (b. 1964), Jarman's long-time partner and loyal caretaker of Prospect Cottage.

2019

– *Derek Jarman Protest!*, retrospective exhibition at the Irish Museum of Modern Art, Dublin, in collaboration with the Manchester Art Gallery, which takes over the exhibition in 2021–2022.

2020

– The Art Fund launches a successful crowdfunding campaign to acquire, protect and bring Prospect Cottage to life. The first artists in residence are welcomed in 2023.

– Exhibition *Derek Jarman: My Garden's Boundaries Are the Horizon*, The Garden Museum, Londres

2021

– Exhibition *Derek Jarman. Dead Souls Whisper (1986–1993)*, Centre d'art contemporain d'Ivry – le Crédac, Ivry-sur-Seine.

– Exhibition view, *Derek Jarman Protest!*, Irish Museum of Modern Art, Dublin, 2019

Untitled (Slade Entrance Exam), 1962

Landscape, 1961

Old Mortality, 1982

Derek Jarman in front of *Self Portrait*, 1959

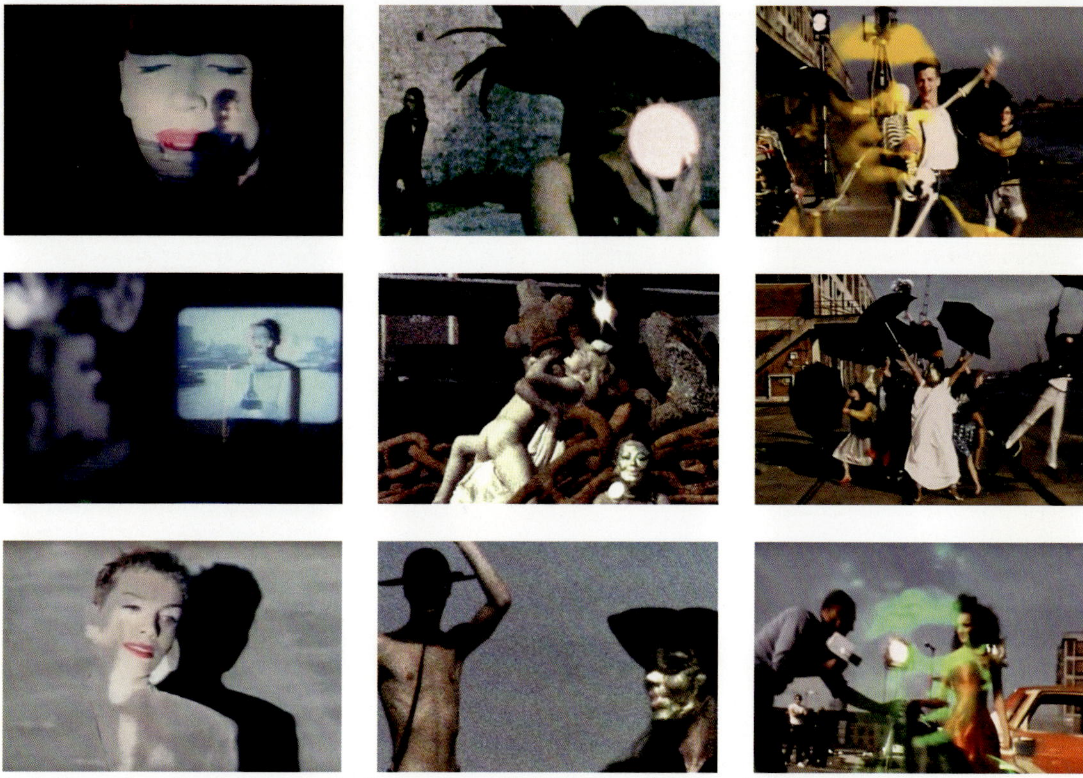

Music videos for *Every Time We Say Goodbye* (1990) by Annie Lenox, *Witches' Songs* (1979) by Marianne Faithfull and *Ask* (1986) by The Smiths

Exhibition view, *Queer*, Filmmuseum, Potsdam, 1993

DEREK JARMAN'S WRITINGS FIRST EDITIONS

- *A Finger in the Fishes Mouth*, Bettiscombe Press, Bridport 1972; Test Centre Publications, London 2014
- *Dancing Ledge*, Quartet Books, London 1984; Vintage, London 2021
- *The Last of England/Kicking the Pricks*, Constable, London 1987; Vintage, London 1996
- *Modern Nature: The Journal of Derek Jarman*, Century, London 1991; Vintage, London 1992
- *At Your Own Risk. A Saint's Testament*, Hutchinson, London 1992; Vintage, London 1993
- *Chroma: A Book of Colour – June '93*, Century, London 1994; Vintage, London 1995
- *Derek Jarman's Garden*, photographs by Howard Sooley, Thames & Hudson, London 1995
- *Smiling in Slow Motion: Journals, 1991–1994*, Century, London 2000; Vintage, London 2001
- *Derek Jarman's Sketchbooks*, Thames & Hudson, London 2013
- *Through the Billboard Promised Land Without Ever Stopping*, House Sparrow Press, London 2022
- *Pharmacopoeia: A Dungeness Notebook*, Vintage, London 2022

SCRIPTS AND FILM-RELATED BOOKS

- *War Requiem*, Faber & Faber, London 1989
- *Caravaggio*, Thames & Hudson, London 1986
- *Queer Edward II*, BFI Publishing, London 1991
- *Wittgenstein*, BFI Publishing, London 1993
- *Blue*, BFI Publishing, London 1993
- *Up in the Air: Collected Film Scripts*, Vintage, London 1996
- *Jubilee (The Play)*, Oberon Books, Islington 2017

SOME DATES RELATING TO HIV/AIDS IN THE UNITED KINGDOM**

1981
12 December: a 49-year-old gay man dies at the Royal Brompton Hospital from an AIDS-related illness, becoming the first person to die from the disease in the UK.

1982
Creation of the Terrence Higgins Trust, named after one of England's first AIDS victims.

1986
Broadcast on Channel 4 of *Bright Eyes* by experimental film-maker and video artist Stuart Marshall; the film deconstructs the factors linking discrimination, scientific analysis, media treatment, homophobia and AIDS-related illnesses.

1987
Publication of *And the Band Played On: Politics, People, and the AIDS Epidemic* by Randy Shilts (Penguin Books, London): this account of the early years of AIDS became a TV film adapted in 1993 by Roger Spottiswoode.

The UK's first needle exchange centre opens in Dundee.

Publication of Simon Watney's articles 'The Spectacle of AIDS' and 'Photography and AIDS' The film *This Is Not An AIDS Advertisement* by English film-maker Isaac Julien is a response to the prevailing puritanism.

1988
Section 28 comes into force, prohibiting any local authority from promoting a positive image of homosexuality. A demonstration under the slogan 'Stop Section 28' organised on 20 February 1988 in Manchester, confirmed the city's status as a forerunner of queer politics and culture.

1990
Watney and others found the OutRage! group, which engages in radical non-violent direct action and civil disobedience.

1991
Freddie Mercury becomes the first UK celebrity to die of an AIDS-related illness, the day after he reveals he has AIDS.

1993
The UK Coalition of People Living with HIV and AIDS is launched in London, just as the Department of Health cuts funding for the Terrence Higgins Trust by two-thirds without explanation.

** Chronology based on that written for the publication of Élisabeth Lebovici's *Ce que le sida m'a fait. Art et activisme à la fin du XXe siècle*, JRP|Editions, Geneva 2021, available at http://www.cequelesidamafait.com, and resources from the websites of Each Other and *The Independent*.

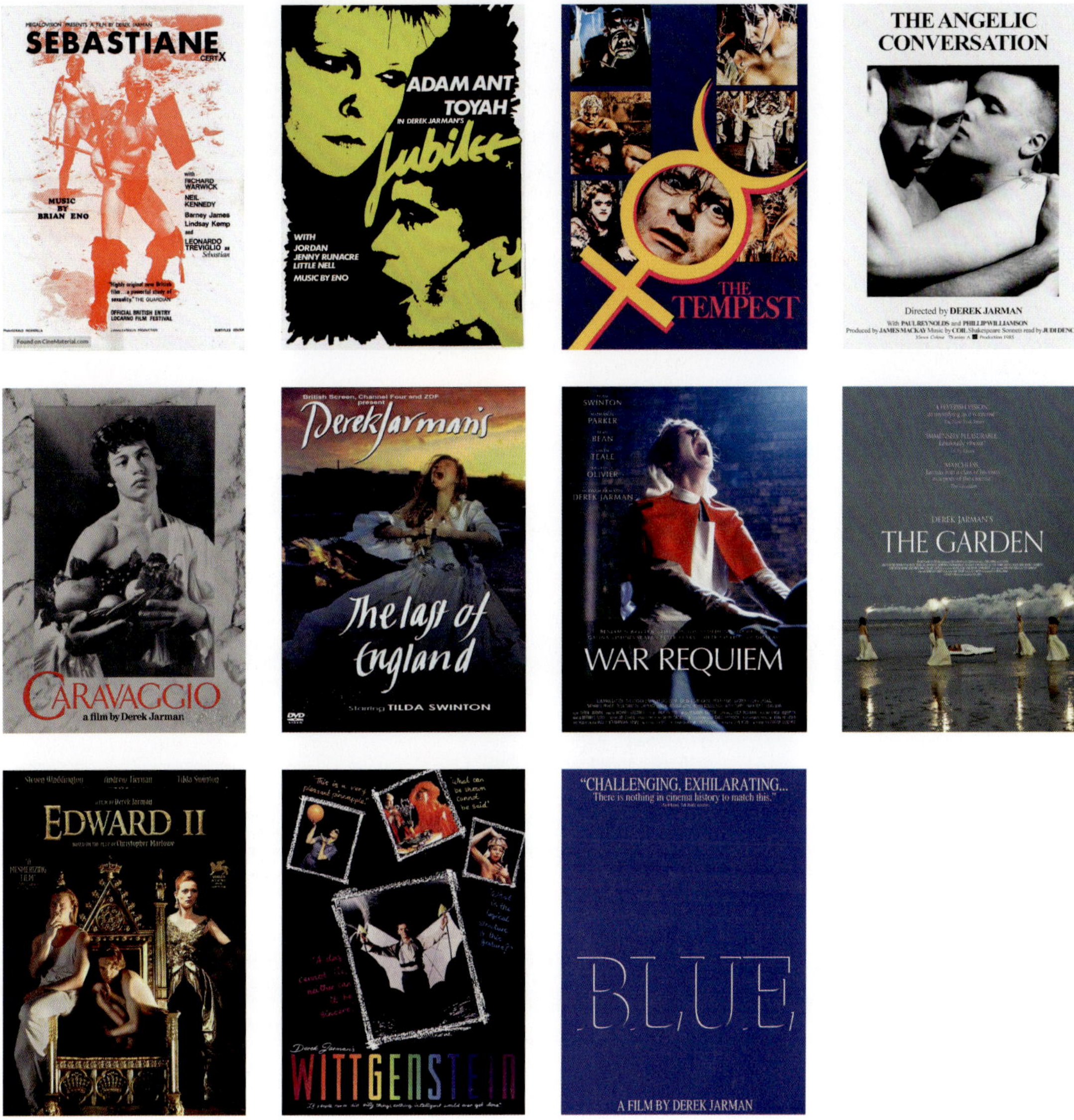

Posters for Jarman's films, 1976–1993

LIST OF WORKS AND ILLUSTRATIONS

1
Derek Jarman wearing his *Money Cape* in front of his Bankside studio, London, 1970
Photograph: Raymond Dean

2–3
Derek Jarman with his *Sky Capes* on the wall, Bankside studio, London, 1971
Photograph: Raymond Dean

4–5
Sloane Square: A Room of One's Own, 1974–1976
Super-8 film, colour and black & white, 8'19"; filmed with Guy Ford

6–7
Derek Jarman addressing the audience, National Review of Live Art Performance, Third Eye Centre Glasgow, October 1989

8
Derek Jarman during the making of the *Queer Paintings*, Richard Salmon studio, 59 South Edwardes Square, London, 1992
Photograph: Howard Sooley

12–14
Derek Jarman in *Blue*, 1993

17
Outside wall of Prospect Cottage adorned with *The Sun Rising* (1633) by John Donne, 2019
Photograph: Claire Le Restif

19
Luke Fowler
Being Blue (Working Title), 2024 (detail)
Stills from a 16mm film shot during a residency at Prospect Cottage, Dungeness, 2023

20
Prospect Cottage, Dungeness, 2019
Photographs: Claire Le Restif

23
Derek Jarman in Claude Monet's garden, Giverny, 1993
Photograph: Howard Sooley

25–43
Exhibition views, *Derek Jarman. Dead Souls Whisper (1986–1993)*, Centre d'art contemporain d'Ivry – le Crédac, Ivry-sur-Seine, 2021

44
Derek Jarman (background) and his assistants during the making of the *Queer Paintings*, Richard Salmon studio, 59 South Edwardes Square, London, 1992; left: Piers Clemett, centre: Peter Filligham
Photograph: Howard Sooley

47
Derek Jarman working with tar, c. 1991

50
GBH Series II, 1983–1984
Mixed media on canvas, 289.6 × 241.3 cm
Private Collection

52
GBH Series I, 1983–1984
Mixed media on canvas, 289.6 × 241.3 cm
Private Collection

57
Canonisation of Derek Jarman as Saint Derek of Dungeness by the Sisters of Perpetual Indulgence, Prospect Cottage, Dungeness, September 1991
Photograph: Howard Sooley

59–65
Exhibition views, *Queer*, Manchester City Art Gallery, Manchester, 1992
59: photograph by Howard Sooley

66
Derek Jarman during the making of the *Queer Paintings*, 1992
Photograph: Howard Sooley

70
Wyndham Lewis
Portrait of the Artist as the Painter Raphael, 1921
Oil on canvas, 76.3 × 68.6 cm
Collection Manchester Art Gallery, Manchester

Self-Portrait (After Wyndham Lewis), 1959
Oil on canvas, 63 × 49 cm

71
Paul Nash
Nocturnal Landscape, 1938
Oil on canvas, 76.5 × 101.5 cm
Collection Manchester Art Gallery, Manchester

Avebury Series no. 4, 1973
Oil on canvas, 122 × 122 cm
Collection Northampton Museum and Art Gallery, Northampton

73
British Scum, 1987
Oil and mixed media on canvas, 30.5 × 25.4 cm
Collection Manchester Art Gallery, Manchester

75
Grievous Bodily Harm, 1986
Oil and mixed media on canvas, 46.3 × 35.5 cm
Collection Manchester Art Gallery, Manchester

77
EIIR, 1992
Oil and photocopy on canvas, 251.4 × 179 cm

78
Tragedy, 1992
Oil and photocopy on canvas, 251.4 × 149 cm

79
Blood, 1992
Oil and photocopy on canvas, 251.4 × 179 cm

80
To Have and To Hold, 1992
Oil and photocopy on canvas, 251.4 × 179 cm

81
40% of British Women, 1992
Oil and charcoal on photocopy on canvas, 251.4 × 149 cm

82
Blind Date, 1992
Oil and photocopy on canvas, 251.4 × 149 cm

83
Now We've All Been Screwed by the Cabinet, 1992
Oil on canvas, 251.4 × 149 cm

85
Time, 1992
Oil and photocopy on canvas, 251.4 × 179 cm

86–87
Sold Out, 1992
Oil and photocopy on canvas, 61 × 101.5 cm

89
Dead Angels, 1992
Oil and photocopy on canvas, 251.4 × 149 cm

90
Negative Image, 1992
Oil and photocopy on canvas, 251.4 × 149 cm

91
Spread the Plague, 1992
Oil and photocopy on canvas, 251.4 × 149 cm

93
Letter to the Minister, 1992
Oil and photocopy on canvas, 251.4 × 149 cm

94
Priest, 1992
Oil on canvas, 101.5 × 61 cm

95
Queer, 1992
Oil on canvas, 251.4 × 179 cm
Collection Manchester Art Gallery, Manchester

96
Oh Zone, 1992
Oil on canvas, 213.5 × 213.5 cm

97
Acid Rain, 1992
Oil on canvas, 213.5 × 213.5 cm

99–101
Love Sex Death, 1992
Oil on canvas, triptych, 51 × 61 cm each

102
Landscape, 1991
Oil on canvas, 40.6 × 45.7 cm
Samuel Ellis Scheinman Collection

103
Landscape, 1991
Oil on canvas, 40.6 × 45.7 cm
Private Collection

105
Fuck Me Blind, 1993
Oil on canvas, 251.4 × 179 cm
Julia Muggenburg Collection

106
Toxo, 1992
Oil and photocopy on canvas, 251.4 × 179 cm

107
Sick, 1992
Oil and photocopy on canvas, 251.4 × 179 cm

108
Kiss, 1992
Oil on canvas, 101.5 × 61 cm

109
KY, 1992
Oil and photocopy on canvas, 101.5 × 61 cm

111
Blackmail, 1992
Oil and photocopy on canvas, 101.5 × 61 cm

112
True Blue, 1992
Oil and photocopy on canvas, 101.5 × 61 cm
Julien Sands Collection

113
Poofs, 1992
Oil and photocopy on canvas, 101.5 × 61 cm

114
AIDS Blood, 1992
Oil on canvas, 101.5 × 61 cm

115
Positive, 1992
Oil and photocopy on canvas, 251.4 × 149 cm

116
Derek Jarman, Prospect Cottage, Dungeness, Summer 1992
Photograph: Howard Sooley

119
Outline for the planting of Derek Jarman's garden in Dungeness, from the notebook *Garden Book 1*, 1989
Notebook, 20.3 × 20.3 cm
Private Collection

125
Prospect Cottage, Dungeness, 1992
Photograph: Howard Sooley

126–127
Film still from *The Garden*, 1990

129
Prospect Cottage, Dungeness, 2018
Photographs: Cy Lecerf Maulpoix

131
Film stills from *The Clearing* (1993) by Alexis Bistikas

133
Derek Jarman, Prospect Cottage, Dungeness, 1992
Photograph: Howard Sooley

135
Prospect Cottage, Dungeness, 1992
Photograph: Howard Sooley

136
Prospect Cottage, Dungeness, 2021
Photograph: Benoît Piéron

137
Prospect Cottage, Dungeness, 2021
Photographs: Richard Deacon

138–139
Derek Jarman, Prospect Cottage, Dungeness, Summer 1992
Photograph: Geraint Lewis

140–143
Prospect Cottage, Dungeness, 2019
Photographs: Claire Le Restif

144–146
Luke Fowler
Being Blue (Working Title), 2024 (detail)
Stills from a 16mm film shot during a residency at Prospect Cottage, Dungeness, 2023

147
Prospect Cottage, Dungeness, 1992
Photograph: Howard Sooley

149
Nightlife, 1987
Oil and mixed media on canvas, 44.5 × 27.9 × 10.2 cm

150
Untitled, 1989
Mixed media, 23.5 × 13.97 × 11.43 cm

151
A PLANT, 1988
Oil and mixed media on canvas, 54 × 35.5 × 8 cm

152
Dead Souls Whisper, 1987
Oil and mixed media on canvas, 30.5 × 25.4 cm

153
Untitled, 1987
Oil and mixed media on canvas, 30.5 × 25.4 cm

155
Untitled (Bone, Face and Cross), 1988
Oil and mixed media on canvas, 45.7 × 25.4 cm

156
Untitled, 1988
Oil and mixed media on canvas, 41.2 × 25.4 cm

157
Archaeology, 1988
Oil and mixed media on canvas, 35.5 × 25.4 cm

158
Untitled (Gold Bible), 1990
Oil and mixed media on canvas, 30.8 × 25.4 cm

159
At the Fifth Quarter of the Globe, 1988
Oil and mixed media on canvas, 45.7 × 35.5 cm

161
Jumble Sale, 1990
Oil and mixed media on canvas, 30.8 × 25.4 cm

162
Untitled (Comb), 1989
Oil and mixed media on canvas, 41.3 × 35.5 cm

163
Untitled (Technico), 1989
Oil and mixed media on canvas, 40.6 × 35.5 cm

164
CMV Virus (Sight Oh Megalo), 1992
Oil on canvas with black metal foil, 35.6 × 25.4 cm

165
Prospect (Et in Arcadia Ego), 1992
Oil on canvas with black metal foil, 35.6 × 25.4 cm

167
Death is All Things We See Awake, 1991
Tar and mixed media on canvas, 50.8 × 38.1 cm

168
The Bridge of Sighs, 1987
Oil and mixed media on canvas, 36.1 × 30.5 cm

169
Every Thought, 1987
Oil and mixed media on canvas, 30.5 × 25.4 cm

171
Untitled (Red Crucified Figure), 1991
Oil and mixed media on canvas, 51.5 × 36.2 × 8 cm

172
The Common Prayer, 1989
Tar and mixed media on canvas, 40.6 x 35.5 cm

173
Flesh Tint, 1990
Oil and mixed media on canvas, 36.1 × 30.8 cm

175
Household God VI (Nelson), 1989
Mixed media, 27.6 × 17.8 × 10.2 cm

176
Household God V (Molière), 1989
Mixed media, 17.1 × 9.5 × 11.1 cm

177
Household God III (Wagner), 1989
Mixed media, 19 × 12.5 × 9 cm

178
Household God I (Handel), 1989
Mixed media, 26 × 18.4 × 10.2 cm

179
Household God II (Mozart), 1989
Mixed media, 22 × 13 × 11 cm

180
On the set of *The Garden*, 1990
Photograph: James Mackay

182
James Mackay during the production of the opera *L'ispirazione* directed by Derek Jarman, Florence, 1988

185
On the set of *The Garden*, 1990
Photographs: James Mackay

186
In the Shadow of the Sun, 1972–1974
Super-8 film, colour, 49'24"

188
Imagining October, 1984
Super-8 film, colour, 27'

196
Exhibition view, *Portraits dans le temps*, Luma Arles, Arles, 2021

Exhibition view, *Derek Jarman: Brutal Beauty*, Serpentine Gallery, London, 2008

197
Sulphur, 1975
Super-8 film, colour, 15'15"

201
Derek Jarman showering Leonardo Treviglio on the set of *Sebastiane*, 1976
Photograph: Gerald Incandela

205
Bed (IV), 1988–1989
Mixed media on wooden frame, 231.5 × 134 × 25 cm

Bed (VII), 1988–1989
Mixed media on wooden frame, 231.5 x 134 x 25 cm

207
Studio Bankside, 1972
Super-8 film, colour and black & white, 6'47"

209
Tarot (The Magician), 1973
Super-8 film, colour, 7'39"; with Christopher Hobbs, Gerald Incandela

210
Journey to Avebury, 1973
Super-8 film, colour, 13'29"

213
Derek Jarman with a cast of his face made by Christopher Hobbs, 1980

215
Death Dance, 1973
Super-8 film, colour, 15'27"; with Christopher Hobbs (The Death), Gerald Incandela, Tim Spain, Robin Wall and Kevin Whitney

216
Sloane Square: A Room of One's Own, 1974–1976
Super-8 film, colour and black and white, 8'19"; filmed with Guy Ford; with Guy Ford, Alasdair McGaw, Graham Cracker and Derek Jarman

217, 221
At Low Tide, 1972
Super-8 film, colour, 6'53"; filmed with Marc Balet; with Andrew Logan, Bente Lohse
Costumes and props: Christopher Hobbs

227
Art & the Pose, 1977
Super-8 film, black and white, 8'11"; with Jean-Marc Prouveur and Gerald Incandela

229
Derek Jarman as Miss Crêpe Suzette, laureate of Alternative Miss World 1975, London, 1975
Photograph: Marc Balet

231
Simon Fisher Turner and Derek Jarman in *Blue*, 1993

235
Jordan's Dance, 1977
Super-8 film, colour, 16'29"

239
Derek Jarman and Tilda Swinton, Berlin, c. 1986

251
Derek Jarman's studio during the making of the *Queer Paintings*, 1992
Photographs: Simon Watney

253
Images from the documentary *Hating Peter Tatchell* by Christopher Amos, 2021

255
Derek Jarman during a march organised by OutRage!, London, 6 February 1992

256
Derek Jarman in front of *After Poussin's Inspiration of a Poet*, Priory Road Studio, 1966–1967
Photograph: Raymond Dean

258
The Jarman family at Dancing Ledge, 1956

Derek Jarman, David Hockney and Ossie Clark at Jarman's birthday party, Sloane Square, London, 1968

Derek Jarman, Lisson Gallery, London, 1969

Sketch for the set of *Jazz Calendar*, 1967

Rehearsal for *Jazz Calendar*, 1968, Royal Opera House, Covent Garden, London

Derek Jarman on the set of *The Devils* (1970) by Ken Russel, Pinewood Studios

259
Set by Derek Jarman for an act of *The Rake's Progress* staged by Ken Russell, Florence, 1982

Michael Clark dancing in Jarman's exhibition at the Institute of Contemporary Arts, London, 1982
Film still from the Super-8 film *ICA*, 1982

Image from the documentary *Derek Jarman. A Portrait* (1990) filmed by Mark Kidel

Exhibition view, *Derek Jarman Protest!*, Irish Museum of Modern Art, Dublin, 2019

260
Untitled (Slade Entrance Exam), 1962
Oil on canvas, 63 × 76.5 cm
Private Collection

Landscape, 1961
Oil on canvas, 122 × 92 cm
Private Collection

Old Mortality, 1982
Oil on canvas, 121.9 × 86.4 cm

Derek Jarman in front of *Self Portrait*, 1959
Photograph published in *Watford Advertiser*, 1960

261
Music videos for *Every Time We Say Goodbye* (1990) by Annie Lenox, *Witches' Songs* (1979) by Marianne Faithfull and *Ask* (1986) by The Smiths

Exhibition view, *Queer*, Filmmuseum, Potsdam, 1993

263
Posters for Jarman's films, 1976–1993

267
On the set of *The Garden*, 1992

272
Derek Jarman as Saint Derek of Dungeness, Prospect Cottage, Dungeness, September 1991
Photograph: Howard Sooley

COLLECTIONS AND COURTESIES

Basilisk Communications: p. 12–14, 126–127, 231, 267
Keith Collins Will Trust & Amanda Wilkinson Gallery, London: p. 91, 94, 96, 97, 99–101, 111, 113, 115, 149–179
Keith Collins Will Trust for all the artworks by Derek Jarman: p. 50, 52, 70b, 71b, 73, 75, 77–115, 119, 260
Luma Foundation: p. 4–5, 186, 188, 197, 207, 209, 210, 215, 216, 217, 221, 227, 235
Manchester Art Gallery/Bridgeman Images/© Wyndham Lewis Memorial Trust: p. 70t
Manchester Art Gallery/Bridgeman Images: p. 71t

PHOTO CREDITS

Marc Balet: p. 229; Keith Collins Will Trust: p. 70b, 73, 75, 78, 80, 81, 82, 83, 89, 90, 91, 94, 96, 97, 99–101, 102, 103, 108, 109, 111, 112, 113, 114, 115, 149–179, 213, 259, 260tr/b, 261t, 263; Liam Daniel: p. 12–14, 126–127, 231, 267; Richard Deacon: p. 137; Raymond Dean: p. 1, 2–3, 256, 258r; Marc Domage: p. 25–43, 196t; D.R.: p. 47, 119, 131, 239, 253, 258l; Luke Fowler: p. 19, 144–146; Pia Goddard: p. 261b; Gerald Incandela: p. 201; Claire Le Restif: p. 17, 20, 140–143; Cy Lecerf Maulpoix: p. 129; Geraint Lewis: p. 138–139; James Mackay: p. 180, 185; Manchester Art Gallery: p. 60–65, 70t, 71t, 73, 75, 77, 79, 85, 86–87, 93, 95, 106, 107, 260tl; Manchester Art Gallery/Andrew Brooks: p. 50, 52, 105; Northampton Museum and Art Gallery: p. 71b; Benoît Piéron: p. 136; Gordon Rainsford: p. 255; Serpentine Galleries/Sylvain Deleu: p. 196b, 205; Howard Sooley: p. 8, 23, 44, 57, 59, 66, 116, 125, 133, 135, 147, 272; University of Bristol: p. 6–7; Simon Watney: p. 251; Leland Wheeler: p. 182.

On the set of *The Garden*, 1992

Nizo

GLOSSARY OF NAMES

Kenneth Anger (1927–2023)
American underground experimental film-maker, actor and author. Beginning in 1937, he produced almost 40 works exclusively in the medium of short films. He has been called 'one of America's first openly gay film-makers', with several films released before homosexuality was legalised in the US.

Helmut Berger (1944–2023)
Austrian actor. Seen as a sex symbol and pop icon of the late 1960s and 1970s, he is best known for his work with Luchino Visconti.

Jack Birkett (1934–2010)
British dancer, mime artist, actor and singer, best known for his work on stage as a member of Lindsay Kemp's theatre company, and as an actor in Jarman's films (*Jubilee, The Tempest, Caravaggio, The Garden*).

Alf Bold (1946–1993)
German actor and film critic. For many years he was involved in organising the Forum section of the Berlin International Film Festival and programming the Kino Arsenal in Berlin.

Don Boyd (b. 1948)
Scottish film director, producer, screenwriter and novelist. He produced two of Jarman's films – *The Tempest* and *War Requiem* – as well as co-producing *The Last of England.*

Stan Brackhage (1933–2003)
American film-maker. He is considered to be one of the most important figures in 20th-century experimental film.

Marek Budzynski (b. 1958)
British director, editor and producer.

Pierre Clementi (1942–1999)
French actor and director. He directed some 15 short and medium-length films and appeared in a number of feature films, notably under the direction of Pier Paolo Pasolini, Luchino Visconti, Luis Buñuel, Glauber Rocha and Jacques Rivette.

Jean Cocteau (1889–1963)
French poet, playwright, novelist, designer, film-maker, visual artist and critic. He was a leading figure of the Surrealist, avant-garde and Dadaist movements, and an influential figure in early 20th-century art and culture.

Keith Collins (1964–2018)
British actor. He shared the last eight years of Jarman's life, appearing in his films *The Garden, Edward II* and *Wittgenstein* under his stage name, Kevin Collins.

David Curtis (b. 1942)
British film curator and writer. He was film officer at the Arts Council of Great Britain (1977–2000), and is the author of *Experimental Cinema* (Studio Vista, 1970) and *A History of Artists Film and Video in Britain* (BFI, 2006).

John Du Cane (b. 1949)
Also known as Rishi, he is a British writer and film-maker. He made 34 films between 1972 and 1975 during a brief period of activity in which he was associated with the London Film-Makers' Co-op.

Terry Eagleton (b. 1943)
English literary theorist, critic and intellectual, best known for *Literary Theory: An Introduction* (1983). Other publications include *The Illusions of Postmodernism* (1996) and *After Theory* (2003).

Marianne Faithfull (b. 1946)
Internationally acclaimed English rock singer, actress and author. Jarman directed the music videos for *Broken English*, *Witches' Song* and *The Ballad of Lucy Jordan* (all 1979).

Simon Field
British film curator and producer. He was the director of film at the Institute of Contemporary Arts in London (1988–1996) and director of the International Film Festival Rotterdam (1996–2004).

Guy Ford
British assistant director and producer. He is best known for assisting Jarman on *Sebastiane, Jubilee* and *The Tempest.*

Diamanda Galás (b. 1955)
American musician, singer-songwriter, visual artist and soprano. She has campaigned for AIDS education and the rights of the people with AIDS.

Peter Gidal (b. 1946)
British writer, theorist and film-maker. He was an active member of the London Film-Makers' Co-op and was its cinema programmer from 1971 to 1974. His numerous writings on film and art include *Andy Warhol: Films and Paintings* (1971) and *Materialist Film* (1989).

Liam Gillick (b. 1964)
British artist. He was one of the Young British Artists, a loose group of visual artists who first began to exhibit together in London in 1988 and who dominated the British art during the 1990s.

Peter Greenaway (b. 1942)
British film director, screenwriter and artist. His films are noted for the distinct influence of Renaissance and Baroque painting, and Flemish painting in particular, as well as for their soundtracks.

Erika and Ulrich Gregors (b. 1934 and 1932)
German film curators, founders of the Kino Arsenal and the International Forum of Young Cinema of the Berlinale. By bringing countless historical film milestones to Berlin they shaped cinema discourse in post-war Germany.

Birgit Hein (1942–2023)
German film-maker and film scholar. With the structural films that she started making in 1966, as well as her performances, documentary films, essays and film study publications, she is considered an indisputable pioneer of German underground and experimental film.

Wilhelm Hein (b. 1940)
German film-maker Together with his then wife Birgit Hein, he was an important pioneer of experimental film in Germany from the 1960s onwards.

Richard Heslop (b. 1961)
British director of music videos and films. He has produced videos for artists including Queen, The Cure and New Order. His experimental film *The Raft of the Medusa* – based on a radio play by Simon Armitage, created in association with BBC Radio 4 and aired on 12 April 2015 – is a tribute to Jarman.

Christopher Hobbs (1941–2024)
British painter, sculptor and set designer, who worked with Jarman on many of his films including *Sebastiane*, *Caravaggio* – for which he made copies of Caravaggio paintings – and *Edward II.*

David Hockney (b. 1937)
British artist and art theorist. He is one of the most influential painters of the 20th century. He studied at London's Royal College of Art at the same time as Jarman.

Danièle Huillet (1936–2006) and
Jean-Marie Straub (1933–2022)
French film-makers who together made two dozen films between 1963 and 2006. Their films are distinguished by their rigorous, intellectual style and their radical politics.

Takahiko Iimura (1937–2022)
Japanese avant-garde film-maker and fine artist. He is considered one of the pioneers of experimental and independent film-making in Japan.

Isaac Julien (b. 1960)
British artist and film-maker. He co-founded Sankofa Film and Video Collective in 1983, and was a founding member of Normal Films in 1991. He curated the exhibition *Derek Jarman: Brutal Beauty*, Serpentine Gallery, London, 2008.

Jeff Keen (1923–2012)
British pioneer of experimental film, and an artist and poet, whose rapid-fire animations, multiple screen projections and raucous performances redefined multimedia art in Britain. Keen was a veteran of the Second World War, and his work powerfully evokes the violence, colour, speed and noise of the 20th century.

Kurt Kren (1929–1998)
Austrian avant-garde film-maker. He is best known for his association with the Viennese Actionists, although he later returned to his structural roots.

Malcolm Le Grice (b. 1940)
British artist, known for his avant-garde film work. He was one of the founders of the London Film-Makers' Co-op workshop in 1966.

Spencer Leigh (b. 1963)
British actor and director. He appeared in several films directed by Jarman, including *Caravaggio*, *The Last of England*, *War Requiem* and *The Garden.*

Andrew Logan (b. 1945)
English sculptor, performance artist, jeweller and portrait artist. He founded Alternative Miss World in 1972, which he ran until 2018. Jarman filmed Logan and his work in several of his early Super-8 films.

Silvana Mangano (1930–1989)
Italian actress. She starred in films by some of the greatest directors of her time, including Vittorio De Sica, Luchino Visconti, Pier Paolo Pasolini, René Clément and later David Lynch.

John Maybury (b. 1958)
English film-maker and artist. In the 1980s he produced a number of short films and music videos, before moving on to feature films from 1988, including biopics on the life of painter Francis Bacon and Welsh poet Dylan Thomas.

Laura Mulvey (b. 1941)
British feminist film theorist. She is best known for her essay *Visual Pleasure and Narrative Cinema* (1973) which helped to bring the term 'male gaze' into film criticism, and eventually into common parlance. She was also prominent as an avant-garde film-maker in the 1970s and 1980s.

Lynda Myles (b. 1947)
British writer and producer. She is best known for her work as the director of the Edinburgh International Film Festival.

Orange Juice
Scottish jangle pop band featuring Edwyn Collins. They were founded in Glasgow as the Nu-Sonics in 1976, before becoming Orange Juice in 1979.

Sergei Parajanov (1924–1990)
Armenian film-maker musician, visual artist and painter. His film *The Color of Pomegranates* (1969) is considered a landmark in the history of cinema.

Ron Peck (1948–2022)
British film-maker. Through his six feature films and numerous shorts and documentaries, he was a pioneer in Britain's independent film scene of the 1970s and 1980s. His film *Nighthawks* (1978) is a milestone in LGBTQIA+ cinema.

Pet Shop Boys
English synth-pop duo formed in London in 1981, consisting of primary vocalist Neil Tennant and keyboardist Chris Lowe. Jarman directed music videos for *It's a Sin* (1987) and *Rent* (1987), and created a series of film backdrops for their first world tour, as well as directing it.

Sally Potter (b. 1949)
English film director and screenwriter, performance artist and theatre director. She has made both experimental film and dance pieces. She has directed ten feature films, including *Orlando* (1992), starring Tilda Swinton, *The Man Who Cried* (2000), and *Ginger & Rosa* (2012).

Genesis Breyer P-Orridge (1950–2020)
English singer-songwriter, musician, poet, performance artist, visual artist and occultist. P-Orridge was the founder of the COUM Transmissions artistic collective and lead vocalist of seminal industrial band Throbbing Gristle. P-Orridge also fronted the experimental pop rock band Psychic TV.

Vanessa Redgrave (b. 1937)
English actress and activist. In a career spanning more than six decades, she has appeared in films directed by Michelangelo Antonioni, Sidney Lumet, Joseph Losey, Ken Russel, James Ivory and Brian de Palma.

Lis Rhodes (b. 1942)
British artist and feminist film-maker. She was cinema programmer at the London Film-Makers' Co-op from 1975 to 1976. In 1979, she co-founded the feminist film distribution network, Circles, and since 1978 has lectured part-time at the Slade School of Fine Art, University College London.

Jacob Rothschild (1936–2024)
British peer, investment banker and a member of the Rothschild banking family. He was active in several charitable and philanthropic areas, in particular the project to restore Somerset House in London.

Ken Russell (1927–2011)
British film director. He is best known for his Oscar-winning film *Women in Love* (1969), *The Devils* (1971) and The Who's *Tommy* (1975). Russell also directed several films based on the lives of classical music composers, such as Elgar, Delius, Tchaikovsky, Mahler and Liszt.

Manfred Salzgeber (1943–1994)
German actor, film distributor and film producer. He was director of the Panorama section of the Berlin International Film Festival, and a co-founder of the International Forum of Young Cinema Films.

Ferdinando 'Nando' Scarfiotti (1941–1994)
Italian art director and theatre designer. He designed sets for films by Bernardo Bertolucci, Brian De Palma and Luchino Visconti.

Carolee Schneemann (1939–2019)
American experimental visual artist, known for her multi-media works exploring the body, narrative, sexuality and gender.

Paul Sharits (1943–1993)
American visual artist, best known for his work in experimental film-making particularly in what became known as the structural film movement.

Guy Sherwin (b. 1948)
British artist working in film. He was involved with the London Film-Makers' Co-op where he learnt, and then taught, the darkroom arts of printing and processing.

The Smiths
English rock band formed in Manchester in 1982 made up of singer Morrissey, guitarist Johnny Marr, bassist Andy Rourke and drummer Mike Joyce. Jarman directed *The Queen Is Dead*, a short film incorporating The Smiths' songs *The Queen Is Dead*, *Panic* and *There Is a Light That Never Goes Out* (all 1986), as well as the music video for *Ask* (1986).

Spring (Rupert Audley)
British actor featured in *The Last of England*.

Patrick Steede
British film-maker and writer.

Terry-Thomas
(born Thomas Terry Hoar Stevens, 1911–1990)
British actor.

Throbbing Gristle
English music and visual arts group formed in 1975 in Kingston-upon-Hull by Genesis P-Orridge, Cosey Fanni Tutti, Peter Christopherson and Chris Carter. They are widely regarded as pioneers of industrial music. They provided soundtracks for Jarman's *In the Shadow of the Sun* (1972–1974) and *TG Psychic Rally in Heaven* (1981)

Heathcote Williams (1941–2017)
British poet, actor, playwright and political activist. He played the role of Prospero in Jarman's *The Tempest* (1979).

Peter Wollen (1938–2019)
British film theorist and film-maker. His book *Signs and Meaning in the Cinema* (1969) helped to transform the discipline of film studies through the synthesis of the methodology of structuralism and semiotics.

Cerith Wyn Evans (b. 1958)
Welsh conceptual artist, sculptor and film-maker. He served as an assistant to Jarman, with whom he worked on *The Angelic Conversation*, *The Last of England* and *Caravaggio*.

CONTRIBUTORS

Laetitia Chauvin (b. 1977)
French art critic and editor, editor-in-chief of the review *Pleased to meet you* (Semiose éditions) whose eleventh issue was dedicated to Derek Jarman in 2021.

Fiona Corridan (b. 1970)
British art historian. She has been Curator of Art and Design at the Manchester Art Gallery since 2006. With Jon Savage and Seán Kissane, she co-organised the touring exhibition *Derek Jarman Protest!* which, after being shown at the Irish Museum of Modern Art (IMMA) in Dublin, toured to Manchester in 2021–2022.

Richard Deacon (b. 1949)
British sculptor and a winner of the Turner Prize (1987). His work often alludes to anatomical functions or industrial objects.

Simon Fisher Turner (b. 1954)
English musician, songwriter, producer and actor. He recorded several film soundtracks for Jarman, including *Caravaggio*, *The Last of England*, *The Garden* and *Blue*. In 2011, Turner released *Soundtracks for Derek* on Optical Sound, a score composed for Jarman's *Super-8* exhibition at the Julia Stoschek Foundation (Düsseldorf). He continues to perform *Blue* in concerts across Europe.

Luke Fowler (b. 1978)
Scottish artist, film-maker and musician. He received the inaugural Derek Jarman Award in 2008 and was shortlisted for the Turner Prize in 2012 for his debut feature *All Divided Selves*. In 2023, he was one of the first residents invited to Prospect Cottage.

Philip Hoare
British writer, film-maker, and curator. His books include *Leviathan*, winner of the Samuel Johnson Prize. He is co-curator of the digital projects Moby Dick Big Read and Ancient Mariner Big Read. In 2021 he curated *Derek Jarman's Modern Nature* at the John Hansard Gallery, Southampton.

Gerald Incandela (b. 1952)
American artist and photographer.

Claire Le Restif (b. 1967)
French art historian and curator. Since 2003, she has directed Le Crédac – Centre d'art contemporain d'Ivry. In 2021, she organised the exhibition *Derek Jarman. Dead Souls Whisper (1986–1993)*, which led to the rediscovery of Jarman's work in France.

Élisabeth Lebovici (b. 1953)
French art historian, journalist, art critic and feminist and lesbian activist. She is an LGBTQIA+ rights activist, and has spent several years with Act Up-Paris, an experience she recounts in her book *Ce que le sida m'a fait: art et activisme à la fin du XX*[e] *siècle* (JRP|Editions, 2021).

Cy Lecerf Maulpoix (b. 1990)
French writer, translator and activist, committed to climate justice and LGBTQIA+ struggles. His current research is focused on sexual dissidence, environmental issues and techno-criticism. He has published *Écologies déviantes. Voyage en terres queers* (Cambourakis, 2021).

James Mackay (b. 1954)
Scottish independent film producer and curator who worked with Jarman extensively from the 1980s until his death, and produced many of his films, including *The Angelic Conversation*, *The Last of England* and *Blue*.

Marco Martella
Writer, gardener and member of the European Institute of Gardens and Landscapes. Since 2010, he has edited the magazine *Jardins* (Les Pommes sauvages) and published *Le Jardin perdu* by Jorn de Précy (Actes Sud, 2011) and *Jardins en temps de guerre* by Teodor Cerić (Actes Sud, 2014).

Benoît Piéron (b. 1983)
French artist. He creates installations on a variety of themes, including the sensuality of plants, the boundaries of the body and the temporality of waiting rooms. He practices patchwork and existential gardening, and designs wallpaper.

Jon Savage (b. 1953)
English writer, broadcaster and music journalist, best known for his definitive history of the Sex Pistols and punk music, *England's Dreaming* (1991). With Fiona Corridan and Seán Kissane, he co-organised the touring exhibition *Derek Jarman Protest!* which was shown in Manchester in 2021–2022.

Howard Sooley (b. 1963)
British photographer. In 1990, he was commissioned to photograph Jarman at Prospect Cottage and soon became a regular visitor to Dungeness. His photographs illustrated *Derek Jarman's Garden* (Thames & Hudson, 1995).

Tilda Swinton
(born Katherine Matilda Swinton in 1960)
British actress and producer. She began her acting career in 1986 in Jarman's *Caravaggio*, with whom she has made many other films, including *Edward II*, for which she received the Volpi Prize for Best Actress at the 1991 Venice Film Festival. She is also known for her many collaborations with international film-makers such as David Fincher, Wes Anderson, Jim Jarmusch, Bong Joon-ho and George Miller.

Simon Watney (b. 1949)
British writer, art historian, and AIDS activist. He has published *Policing Desire: Pornography, AIDS and the Media* (Routledge, 1986) and *Imagine Hope: AIDS and the Gay Identity* (Routledge, 2000). He co-founded OutRage! in 1990, and in 1995 he was included in *The Independent*'s list of 40 influential gay men.

Amanda Wilkinson
British art dealer. She opened her own gallery in 2017 after a previous 20-year stint as co-owner and director of Wilkinson Gallery. Based in Farringdon, London, her gallery represents an international group of artists, many of whom explore issues of gender.

ACKNOWLEDGEMENTS

We would like to warmly thank the Amanda Wilkinson Gallery, London, the Keith Collins Will Trust and Amanda Wilkinson; Festival d'Automne à Paris and Marie Collin, Francesca Corona, Gérard di Giacomo, Christelle Masure, Pierre Gendronneau, Sara Clément-Colas, Marie-Camille Désard, Clara Guedj, Yoann Doto and Rémi Fort; Basilisk Communications, London, and James Mackay; *Pleased to meet you* (Semiose), Paris, and Laetitia Chauvin, Benoît Porcher; the Luma Foundation, Arles, and Maja Hoffmann, Mustapha Bouhayati, Matthieu Humery and Luz Gyalui; the Pinault Collection – Bourse de Commerce de Paris, Paris, and Martin Bethenod, Cyrus Goberville, Lili Reynaud-Dewar, Yves-Noël Genod, Simon Fisher Turner, Rainier Lericolais; La Fab. – Fonds de dotation agnès b., Paris, and agnès b., Sébastien Ruiz; the Cinéma d'Ivry–Le Luxy and Jean-Jacques Ruttner; Yann Beauvais, Didier Roth-Bettoni, Seán Kissane, Robert Mills, Benoît Piéron; as well as Derek Jarman's assistants: Piers Clemett, Peter Fillingham and Karl Lyndon.

We also thank the Crédac Board members: Martin Bethenod, President; Paula Aisemberg, Jessica Castex, Clément Dirié, Vincent Gonzalvez, Antoine Goudet, Valérie Mavridorakis and Estefanía Peñafiel Loaiza; as well as Jean-Denis Frater, Jérôme Girard and Noemi Martins.

For the publication, we would like to thank the writers, the contributors, the photographers, the collectors and the estates who have helped us, as well as Dominique Bax, Cyril Béghin, Lucinda Francis, Rachael Horsley, Mark Kidel, Aoife Inman, James Mackay, Seán Kissane, Kristen Nelson (CCA Archive), Alexandra Stockley and Amanda Wilkinson.

This publication stems from the exhibition *Derek Jarman. Dead Souls Whisper (1986–1993)*, held at the Centre d'art contemporain d'Ivry – le Crédac from 25 September to 19 December 2021, curated by Claire Le Restif, in collaboration with Amanda Wilkinson and James Mackay.

The exhibition was co-produced with the Festival d'Automne à Paris, and benefited from collaborations with the Keith Collins Will Trust; the Amanda Wilkinson Gallery, London; Basilisk Communications, London; the Luma Foundation, Zurich; and *Pleased to meet you* (Semiose), Paris, as well as from the support of La Fab. Paris.

Centre d'art contemporain d'Ivry – le Crédac

Director and Curator
Claire Le Restif

Reception and School Mediation Officer
Benoît Caut

Mediator
Julia Leclerc

Administrator
Virginie Lyobard

Head of Production and Residency Manager
Sébastien Martins

Head of Communication, Publishing and Curatorial Research
Ana Mendoza Aldana

Head of Public Relations
Lucia Zapparoli

Technical Team
Gwendal Coulon, Timothy Larcher, Colin Thil, Jérémy Rey

Centre d'art contemporain d'Ivry – le Crédac
La Manufacture des Œillets
1, place Pierre Gosnat
94200 Ivry-sur-Seine
https://credac.fr

LE CRÉDAC

Member of the TRAM, DCA and BLA! networks, le Crédac receives support from the City of Ivry-sur-Seine, the Ministry of Culture – Direction régionale des affaires culturelles d'Île-de-France, the Conseil Régional d'Île-de-France and the Conseil Départemental du Val-de-Marne.

PUBLICATION

Editors
Claire Le Restif, with Laetitia Chauvin and Clément Dirié

Contributors
Laetitia Chauvin, Fiona Corridan, Simon Fisher Turner, Philip Hoare, Gerald Incandela, Claire Le Restif, Élisabeth Lebovici, Cy Lecerf Maulpoix, James Mackay, Marco Martella, Jon Savage, Tilda Swinton and Simon Watney

Editorial Coordination
Clément Dirié

Research and Iconography
Laetitia Chauvin

Translations
Martin Richet

Copy Editing and Proofreading
Clare Manchester

Graphic Design
Gavillet & Cie, Geneva
(Vincent Devaud, Tamara Niklaus)

Typeface
Recital, Theinhardt Condensed
(www.optimo.ch)

Colour Separation & Print
Musumeci S.p.A, Quart (Aosta)

Cover
Blackmail, 1992
Courtesy Keith Collins Will Trust & Amanda Wilkinson Gallery, London
Sloane Square: A Room of One's Own, 1974–1976
Courtesy Luma Foundation, Arles

This publication has been supported by the Centre national des Arts plastiques, Paris, the Fondation Pernod Ricard, Paris, the Festival d'Automne à Paris and Amanda Wilkinson Gallery, London.

Fondation d'entreprise Pernod Ricard
FESTIVAL D'AUTOMNE À PARIS

Print in Europe.

PUBLISHED BY

JRP|Editions
Rue des Bains, 39
CH–1205 Geneva
www.jrp-editions.com

ISBN 978-3-03764-588-8

With the Centre d'art contemporain d'Ivry – le Crédac

A French edition is available under the ISBN 978-3-03764-600-7

JRP|Editions publications are available internationally at selected bookstores and from the following distribution partners:

Switzerland
AVA Verlagsauslieferung AG
www.ava.ch

Germany and Austria
JRP|Editions
books@jrp-editions.com

France
Les presses du réel
www.lespressesdureel.com

UK and other European countries, USA, Canada, Asia and Australia
ARTBOOK|D.A.P.
www.artbook.com

Derek Jarman as Saint Derek of Dungeness, Prospect Cottage, September 1991